J
G

Out of
Many Waters

Out of
Many Waters

Jacqueline Dembar <u>Greene</u>

WALKER & COMPANY
NEW YORK

J
G

Passages from Psalm 18 used by permission of the
Jewish Publication Society.

First published in the United States of America
in 1988 by the Walker Publishing Company, Inc.

Published simultaneously in Canada by Thomas Allen & Son
Canada, Limited, Markham, Ontario.

Library of Congress Cataloging-in-Publication Data
Greene, Jacqueline Dembar.
Out of many waters / Jacqueline Dembar Greene.
p. cm.
Bibliography: p.
Summary: Kidnapped from their parents during the Portuguese Inquisition and
sent to work as slaves at a monastery in Brazil, two Jewish sisters attempt to
make their way back to Europe to find their parents, but instead become part of a
group founding the first Jewish settlement in the United States.
ISBN 0-8027-6811-3 (trade).
[1. Jews—Brazil—History—Fiction. 2. Jews—United States—
History—Fiction. 3. Inquisition—Brazil—Fiction.] I. Title.
PZ7.G8340U 1988 [Fic]—dc19 88-1291

Printed in the United States of America

10 9 8 7 6 5 4 3 2 1

Book design by Laurie McBarnette

ACKNOWLEDGEMENTS

This book could not have been written without the extensive collection provided by the American Jewish Historical Society in Waltham, Massachusetts. I am grateful for their assistance and support in researching the history of this period. Heartfelt thanks go to cousin Sue Taranto of California, who painstakingly traced the family roots in Spain and shared with me many of the names used in the book. My deepest appreciation goes to my family, who supported me with love and encouragement through research, writing, writing blocks, and general joys and defeats of creating this book. Especially, my husband Mal, who faithfully read messy drafts and offered his thoughts; son Matthew, who kept track of my progress and urged me on; and son Kenny, whose unfailing enthusiasm led him to read every chapter as it rolled off the typewriter, and who always asked, "But what happens next?" Finally, a special word of recognition to my editor, Jeanne Gardner, who went beyond the required efforts to encourage me and see this book through to publication.

To my ancestors, the Sephardim, who left behind olive branches and carried with them the keys to their empty houses, using them to unlock new doors.

Contents

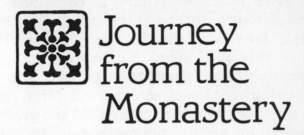 Journey from the Monastery

"Isobel! Maria! Get up!"

Isobel awoke and sat up quickly at Padre Francisco's sharp order. Her neck ached from her cramped position, and her senses were dulled by the intense Brazilian heat.

For eight days Isobel and her sister had traveled on the lumbering, lurching wagon. Often they had walked to lighten the load for the two oxen who pulled it. As always, the girls obeyed the commands of the two friars whom they served.

The friars were traveling from the monastery in Bahia to the newly captured colony at Recife in order to set up a branch of the Inquisition in the name of the Catholic Church of Portugal. Isobel had heard about the workings of the Inquisition from the older children at the monastery. They said the Inquisition leaders had unquestioned powers and forced many Jewish families to convert to the Christian church. Those who refused were burned at the stake. The friars said it was to save their souls.

Still, many *conversos* were suspected of secretly practicing their Jewish religion. Frequently the friars took children from these families and sent them away to be given religious training in the monasteries of distant colonies. Isobel and the girls and boys she had come to know in Bahia had been taken from such families, yet still clung to their Jewish faith.

I am twelve now, Isobel thought, but I was only six years old when I was sent here. I can't remember anything of my family's religion. As the years passed, she longed for her parents more and more, and often had vague dreams of finding them. She knew dreams were only secret wishes, but she had more than that now. She had Maria's plan.

Isobel shaded her eyes from the burning afternoon sun. When she worked in the fields at the monastery, a rest time was allowed during the hottest part of the afternoons. On the trip to Recife, however, the friars tolerated no delays. They set off early each morning and traveled until the flaming orange sun dropped behind the endless fields of sugar cane.

Each night wealthy landowners welcomed the friars and entertained them with lavish dinners and Portuguese wines. Isobel and Maria caught glimpses of the men from the barns where the girls fed and watered the oxen and then made themselves a bed in the sweet-smelling hay.

Isobel preferred soft haystacks to the hard mat in the room at the monastery she shared with Maria and fifteen other girls. On the journey, the sisters were allowed to sleep alone each night, and they talked to each other without danger of being overheard.

It was in the safety of a hayloft that Maria had first told Isobel of her plan. It never would have been possible if they had not been chosen to accompany Padre Francisco and Padre Diego on their mission. At first Isobel was startled by her sister's bold idea, but with a mixture of fear and longing, she dared to hope it could be successful.

She glanced down and saw that Maria was still asleep on the wagon, the hood of her frock pulled over her face to shield her eyes from the sun.

"Maria," she whispered, shaking the older girl's shoulder. She did not want Padre Francisco to become angry because her sister had not obeyed his order to get up. The slightly built friar sat stiffly on the wagon seat, his hands gripping the leather strap attached to the oxen's yoke.

Beside him sat Padre Diego, who was as large and burly as his partner was short and thin. Despite his size, Padre Diego had a gentle manner and was always patient with the children. It was Padre Francisco, with his sharp tongue and ever-present lash, whom Isobel feared.

Maria began to sit up, but not quickly enough. Padre Francisco reached over his shoulder with the long stick he used to prod the oxen and flicked it across Maria's back. It made a whooshing sound as it cut the air and a loud snap as it hit its mark.

Isobel flinched at the sound, knowing well the burning pain it brought. She fought to control the deep-rooted anger that welled up in her. Padre Francisco had no need to whip Maria! Yet, her sister's face reflected no anger or pain, simply an acceptance of the punishment.

"*Perdao, Padre,*" she said automatically to Padre Francisco's ramrod-straight back. "Forgive me."

"It will not be long before we reach Recife," the friar announced. "The oxen are tired and you two are growing lazy. I want you ready to assist the friars at the colony, and some exercise will make you more alert. Get up and walk."

"Yes, Padre." The girls slid off the back of the wagon as it rattled slowly on, rocking the friars from side to side. Padre Diego seemed lulled by the motion as his portly frame rolled in rhythm, but Padre Francisco remained rigid.

Isobel felt as if she were pushing against a wall of heat. She wiped her loose sleeve across her sweaty forehead. "Why can't we ride?" she asked Maria quietly. "I'm too hot to walk."

"I know," Maria said sympathetically. The hair around her face was damp with perspiration and her cheeks were flushed. "Now that the Portuguese have defeated the Dutch, the friars are in a hurry to get to the colony."

"What will they do?" Isobel asked.

"They will establish a court of the Inquisition to decide who is faithful to the Church." She sighed. "Many will pretend to convert just to remain in Recife.

But the Church will make them confess." Her shoulders sagged, as if a weight had been added.

"Are we *conversos?*" Isobel asked.

"Of course we are," Maria said. "That's why the friars took us away. They don't want us to learn about our true religion. But they can't make us forget."

Isobel reached for her sister's hand, pushing back the long sleeve of her coarse brown frock. Why couldn't Maria understand that she had nothing to remember about being Jewish? Six years had passed since she had been sent here. She felt as if she were a lifetime away from her parents and their religion.

She looked at her sister. With a simple rope tied around her waist, her hood pushed back, and brown leather sandals on her feet, she looked like a smaller version of the friars. Her one distinction was the long, dark hair that gently framed her face and then disappeared under the loose frock.

Isobel felt a shock of recognition. I must look like that, too, she thought. She pulled at her hair and let it fall over her shoulders. Padre Francisco would scold her if he noticed, but she did not want to enter Recife looking like a friar.

Padre Diego glanced briefly behind him to be sure Isobel and Maria did not fall too far behind. He nodded encouragingly at them, then turned back to his companion. "How wise the Church was to take these children from their infidel families while they were still young enough to be educated in the Faith. Here there can be no bad examples to corrupt their minds. I believe we can allow ourselves a measure of pride in our work with them."

"Do not give in to the sin of pride," Padre Francisco admonished.

"Amen," Padre Diego muttered. "But remember that the Bible instructs us that if we teach a child in the right way to go, when he is old, he will not depart from the path."

"Thank goodness we are not yet old," Maria whispered defiantly.

The girls trudged on, trying to keep up with the wagon as it pulled up the steep path. A para nut tree had dropped its woody fruit along the edges of the rutted road and, without a word, Maria hid some in her wide sleeves.

With her arms folded across her chest, Maria caught up to the wagon and stealthily reached for a burlap sugar sack which she had packed for the trip. Isobel held it open while her sister let the nuts drop in.

"*O que pasa?*" demanded Padre Francisco, turning on the wagon seat. "What are you doing?" He passed the reins to his partner and climbed down.

"I thought to lighten the load by carrying our things, Padre," Maria said quietly. She closed the open end of the sack and slung it over her shoulder.

"You brought too much from the start!" the friar shouted. "What have you inside?"

Isobel stared at the ground, but Maria dared to look directly at the friar. With false modesty she said, "It holds only women's things."

Isobel understood her sister's ploy. All the friars were notoriously uncomfortable with girls at the monastery. Padre Francisco's face reddened, but Isobel thought it was more from anger than embarrassment.

He snatched the bag from Maria and said scornfully, "Women's things? You are but little girls!"

Maria held Padre Francisco's gaze steadily. Her voice was quiet but firm. "I beg to differ, Padre. I am sixteen now. I am a woman."

There was a moment of silence that seemed a test of who would falter. Maria and the friar stared steadfastly at each other. Finally, the friar gave in .

"Very well," he said, thrusting the unopened bag at Maria. "Don't burden the oxen with your personal items." He turned abruptly and climbed back into the wagon seat, where Padre Diego humbly turned the reins back to him.

Isobel knew her sister was relieved that the friar had not searched the sack. She herself would not have been so clever at deceiving him. Isobel did not know exactly what the sack contained, but she was certain it was more than "women's things," and that Maria would tell her in her own time.

A slight breeze rustled the stalks of sugar cane as the oxen struggled to pull the wagon up a steep rise. Padre Diego now walked beside the animals, coaxing them along in soothing tones.

"I hear the harbor is crowded with ships, and that the Dutch colonists fight like dogs in their desperation to sail for the safety of Amsterdam," Padre Francisco said scornfully. He flicked the switch across the oxen's backs, and they responded with a mournful lowing. "Our government gives them until April 26 to tie up their affairs and depart. That is just a fortnight away. In two weeks' time we will have much holy work to do in dealing with those who remain. Many will pretend to be faithful, but we will discover those who secretly practice their infidel religion."

As the wagon reached the crest of the hill, Isobel felt a cool, moist wind against her face. She hurried to the top and felt her pulse quicken at the sight of the glistening ocean that stretched out ahead. Tall-masted ships crowded the harbor. Farther out to sea, Portuguese ships ringed the coast, their sails marked with huge red crosses, and black cannons pointed ominously from their holds. As if unaware rows of houses nestled at the harbor's edge, and throngs of people in brightly colored clothes dotted the docks.

"Recife!" Isobel breathed out loud in her astonishment.

Maria lifted the hem of her frock and ascended the hill in long strides. She put her arm around Isobel's shoulder and her face took on an animation Isobel had never seen before.

"My plan has to succeed!" Maria whispered breathlessly. "It has to!"

2

Refuge in the Barn

"Disobedient children!" Padre Francisco shouted. "Come back into the wagon!" But his voice seemed to echo from a great distance. Isobel's head was light with the heat and excitement. The view of Recife had changed her. For the first time, she sensed the meaning of freedom. A new emotion stirred in her—a strong feeling of hope.

The oxen pulled the wagon and its four riders easily down the slope, and as they approached the harbor, Isobel's senses awakened to sounds and sights and smells that she had forgotten existed. The air carried the crisp scent of salt and the pungent odor of drying fish. People called and bantered, filling Isobel's ears with a tantalizing din.

"Hot bread! Hot bread!"

A woman's voice trilled, "Tin cups! Wooden bowls! Cups and bowls here!"

"Mama, Mama," pleaded a little girl, "buy me a sweet!"

Colors swirled about Isobel like dancing rainbows. Vivid flags and banners waved overhead. She saw dresses and shawls in bright hues that seemed to announce themselves out loud. How different Recife was from the heavy silence of the monastery and the drab brown of the fields and frocks.

Maria had told Isobel stories of the trumpeters who played in the palace at Lisbon, and now Isobel imagined their thrilling sound. Yes, she thought, if only the harbor had trumpeters, this vision would be complete.

The wagon turned onto a narrow dirt road that curved between the houses. Stones and ruts made it bounce heavily, but Isobel was too absorbed in her surroundings to mind. Shops and stalls brimmed with food and wares. Children ran freely through the street. But when the wagon lurched to a stop in front of a white wooden church, Isobel remembered that she had no place in the flurry of activity around her. She was still under the charge of the friars. There would be no running in the street for her.

Isobel tried to put aside thoughts of the bustling colony as the friars ordered the girls about. "Those wooden crates go upstairs. Move quickly!" They carried papers and books into musty rooms, dragged the friars' heavy trunks to a cubicle on the upper story, and finally led the oxen and wagon to a dilapidated wooden barn at the rear of the building. A flock of chickens flapped up, squawking, as the girls entered.

They released the huge oxen from the heavy yoke and led each one to a stall. They were gentle beasts, but Isobel always took care to stroke their buff-colored hides so they would not become frightened, and to stay clear of the smooth horns that protruded from the sides of their wide heads. The sisters did not speak while feeding and watering the animals, but when their tasks were completed and Isobel stretched out on a bale of hay, Maria gave the first hint of things to come.

"Don't rest yet, Isobel. With all these chickens, I'm sure we can find some eggs." She leaned down and whispered, "We can hide them easily."

"What good will eggs do us?" Isobel blurted out loud. "I can't imagine trying to hide anything so fragile and messy!"

"Don't talk so loud," Maria scolded. "Look down here!" She held up two brown eggs as if they were a prize, and Isobel began to search for more as if it were a game. There were eggs in every loose pile of hay, and in a few minutes they had gathered a full dozen. Maria found a woven basket, lined it with straw, and placed the eggs inside.

"What will we do with them now?" Isobel asked.

"Bring them into the kitchen," came a deep, commanding voice. Isobel was startled. She had not seen Padre Francisco enter the barn. She hoped he hadn't heard her talking about hiding them. Maria was right. She did speak without thinking.

"I want you to help prepare dinner," the friar said. "Hurry along."

"Yes, Padre," Isobel answered obediently. She watched the friar's retreating back as he headed for the church. Maria hid her sugar sack behind an empty grain bin before leaving.

"I shouldn't have let him see us," she complained. "I should have been more careful. We need those eggs, and now we've lost them!" Isobel followed silently, uncertain why the eggs were so important.

The kitchen was a shed-like structure at the rear of the church building. A huge open fireplace with two brick ovens dominated one wall, and a massive oak table in the middle of the room served as a work area. Cool breezes entered through the open window, and the smell of frying fish and fresh bread filled the room.

A corpulent friar with white hair circling a shiny bald spot at the top of his head greeted them at the door. He wore a spotless white apron tied around his frock and it emphasized his expansive stomach.

"Come in, come in," he gestured eagerly. "It is not often that we are blessed with children here. I hope God will forgive me for saying I needed help with dinner, for in truth, the work is finished, but I wanted to be sure you children were properly fed. You are hungry, yes?" He picked up a wooden spoon and stirred a large pot of boiling rice.

"You are safe with old Padre Pão. That's what they call me, Father Bread, for that is the work I do best." He thought for a moment, and then said, "Actually, you *can* do something for me, and keep me from telling a lie. Set out those plates."

Isobel laid out a stack of wooden plates that had been rubbed smooth and shiny from repeated washings, then stepped back shyly to the open doorway. Padre Pão placed a large slice of fried fish, a big spoonful of sticky white rice, and a mixture of boiled squash and tomatoes on each one. Then in one quick movement, he turned from the table to the ovens, removed the thick wooden closures, and slid out four loaves of bread with a long-handled paddle. He tapped each one authoritatively with his fat, pudgy finger. A hollow sound echoed back.

"Perfeito!" he pronounced with glee. He disappeared into the next room with the bread and returned in a moment. He picked up two plates and motioned with his head for the girls to do likewise. Isobel and Maria followed him into the dining room. The table was set simply with wine goblets and eating utensils. No one was in sight. The girls put the plates down carefully and Padre Pão motioned them back to the kitchen with a wave of his hand, while he summoned the other friars.

The girls soon heard prayers uttered in unison coming from the other room. He's not going to give us any supper, after all, Isobel thought with disappointment. Her stomach growled loudly. Just then Padre Pão appeared in the doorway and said, "Eat! Eat! Help yourselves to everything. There is plenty of food and more bread in the ovens. And the eggs are your reward for finding them!" And then he was gone. Isobel had been wrong. Padre Pão really was going to treat them kindly.

"We can keep the eggs!" Maria said, and immediately set a pot of water to boil over the fire while Isobel served up the generous dinner.

"Why are those eggs so important?" Isobel whispered.

Maria dropped the eggs carefully into the bubbling

water. "When they are boiled hard, Isobel, they won't be messy or fragile and you will see how useful they will be!"

The girls removed the last two loaves of bread from the oven and set them aside. "We must save these," Maria explained quietly, and Isobel did not question her. There was more than enough food without the bread and she wasted no time devouring her meal, taking large bites and eating quickly in case Padre Pão changed his mind. When the eggs had boiled several minutes, Maria carefully removed them with a spoon and replaced them in the basket. They did not look any different than when the girls first brought them in.

"Isobel, quickly! Take the bread and the eggs and put them into my bag. Hide it carefully and then come back before you are missed. I will stay here and start cleaning up." Isobel stuffed one last bite of food into her mouth and looked regretfully at the few morsels still left on her plate.

But she did as she was told and dropped the food into the sack without taking the time to examine its contents. She returned to the kitchen, stopping first to draw a bucket of water from the well in case she needed an excuse for her absence.

Padre Pão had things well in hand when she entered, but was pleased with the water. "That is good, child," he said, taking the bucket. "Now you two may go and get some rest. I know it has been a long journey."

Padre Francisco and Padre Diego entered the kitchen.

"Will the children sleep in the barn?" inquired Padre Pão. "We have no space for them in the church."

"Perhaps they should sleep in the kitchen," Padre Francisco said warily. "There are sixteen Dutch ships in the harbor. They sail in the morning with the tide. I think we should keep a closer watch on them."

"They will be safe enough in the barn," said Padre Diego. "After all," he said mockingly, "are you expecting them to book passage to Amsterdam?"

The two friars smiled at each other, and Padre Pão, picking up the joke, began to chuckle softly as the girls turned toward the barn.

3

Maria's Plan

Isobel hurried to keep up with Maria's demands. She drew two large buckets of water from the well and set them aside in the barn. Maria took the para nuts from the sugar sack, and the girls pried open the outer covering and watched ten or twelve nuts fall from each one.

"Now we've got to crack open the shells," Maria said, reaching for a broken tool handle that lay in a corner.

"See if anyone is coming," she ordered. Isobel peered out the door and looked toward the white-painted church.

"It's clear," she reported. Maria gripped the stout wooden handle with both hands and brought it down forcefully. Under repeated blows, the shells gave way, and Isobel removed the oblong, butter-white nuts. She held one up in the dusky light. "It looks a bit like one of Padre Pão's fat little fingers," she observed. Then, holding her hands up to her throat, she made a disgusted face and said, "Now I'll never be able to eat one!" She laughed at her own remark.

"You would be surprised what you are willing to eat when there is nothing but stale biscuits riddled with bugs! Be thankful to God that we have them."

Eat biscuits with bugs? Isobel's laughter faded. The humor of the moment was gone. The tone of Maria's remark bore too much similarity to one of the friar's frequent reprimands. She avoided Maria's eyes. She had only meant to make a joke.

"Take off your things," Maria directed, walking toward the water pails. "We must wash ourselves as best we can, for there will be no fresh water like this for months to come. I even managed to take a bit of soap from the kitchen." Maria pulled a sliver of brown soap from the straw in the egg basket. "Behold a prize fit for a king!" she exulted.

Isobel pulled off her dusty frock and her chemise and stepped into the wooden trough. She gasped while her sister slowly poured the icy well water over her head and down her back. There was excitement and anticipation in everything now. She scrubbed her face and neck, rubbed between her toes, and lathered the grainy soap into her hair. As Maria rinsed her with the second bucket of water, Isobel combed her fingers through her long hair, chasing out every trace of soap.

"Dry yourself with this," Maria said, handing Isobel her chemise. "I have another one for you." No one at the monastery had two of anything. What could Maria mean? She watched in astonishment as Maria opened the sugar sack and brought out a soft white chemise with long sleeves and a deep hem.

"I made it from old linen sheeting," she smiled in answer to Isobel's unspoken question. "That's why I volunteered to work in the laundry."

"The sleeves are so long," Isobel observed.

"Do you remember when Miriam arrived at the monastery last year?" Isobel could not forget the thin, sickly girl. Isobel had not thought she would survive the difficult life there, but surprisingly, Miriam had a strong will and adjusted better than many others.

"She told me that the Dutch women she saw in Recife rolled the cuffs over their dress sleeves. She says they're beautifully embroidered, but I couldn't do that. I always pretended I was mending when I worked on these. Decorations would have given me away." There was a meaningful pause. "I hope our new chemises will help us blend in. We'll need to look like the others soon."

Isobel slipped the clean white chemise over her head. It smelled of strong lye soap and the musty odor of the burlap sack, but Isobel didn't mind. It was the first new thing she had owned. The frocks and sandals handed out at the monastery were always too big for her, no matter how much she grew. Clothes were patched and worn again until there were more patches than whole cloth. She wrapped her arms around Maria's waist and hugged her in silent gratitude.

"Wash out your old chemise and lay it on the grass to dry while I fetch some water for my own bath," Maria said, disengaging herself from Isobel's arms and stepping outside with the empty buckets.

Isobel was wringing out her undergarment when Maria returned. She spread it out, smoothing the wrinkles so it would dry flat, then she turned to the barn to help her sister bathe.

That night the girls nestled into a thick pile of straw, admiring the new chemises. Maria lowered her voice to a whisper, but Isobel heard its bitterness. "For six years we worked in Bahia for the friars, following their orders, weeding and hoeing, cleaning and scrubbing and cooking. We read their Bible and learned their prayers. We saw our friends die of fever, and were whipped time after time, sometimes just for talking to each other. But I knew they couldn't change us. For six years, I never stopped thinking of the moment when you and I would escape."

Her last word echoed through the barn. Escape! The sound took on a life of its own, beckoning Isobel into an unknown world. Escape! The word filled her with excitement. And terror.

In the moonlight that filtered through the open window, Isobel studied her sister's face. "Maria," she whispered, "I am ready to escape with you."

"Tomorrow morning while the friars are still asleep, we must be up before daylight and get to the harbor. Padre Francisco says sixteen Dutch ships lie at anchor, ready to sail with the morning tide. We must get on board one of those ships." Isobel held her breath. "Then you must try to find a place to hide on deck, where there is fresh air. I cannot tell you where, Isobel, so you must look about quickly."

Isobel watched as her sister opened the sugar sack and emptied it of its contents. The oxen wheezed in their stalls and Isobel glanced around nervously. The friars would not come in this late. They never did. Still, she felt uneasy.

Maria unfolded a second sack that had been hidden inside. "This bag will be yours. I'll give you food to last until you are discovered, which you surely will be. Now you know why we needed the eggs." Into Isobel's bag she placed six cooked eggs, a loaf of bread, some nuts, green bananas, and dried beef. Finally she showed Isobel a corked wine bottle. "This is water," she said. "You will have to use it sparingly, perhaps only allowing yourself a few swallows a day. I hope there is enough food."

"It doesn't matter," Isobel sighed. "I am used to being hungry all the time."

"I have made something else for us to wear," Maria said, and Isobel detected a hint of pride in her voice. Maria untied a bundle of white linen and Isobel strained in the pale light to see what it was. Maria listened for the undisturbed sound of crickets chirping and seemed reassured. She spread the items on the floor.

"Miriam spoke often of the Dutch styles when we were alone. Today I saw some women near the harbor and I believe she was right. There's a white collar for each of us and an apron. We'll put them over our frocks and hope that no one looks too closely. At least we can try to look like Dutch girls and blend into the crowd. I am hoping the collars and aprons will make our frocks look more like dresses. What do you think, Isobel?"

Isobel threw her arms around Maria's neck. "I think

you are wonderful!" she said, trying to keep her voice quiet despite her excitement. "And I think we are going to make it to Amsterdam!"

Maria sensed her sister's anxious anticipation. "I've always thought about getting away, from the moment we were taken from our home. Haven't you?"

"Always," Isobel agreed, "but I never knew how."

"When I heard that the friars needed two children to come with them to Recife, I offered to accompany them if they would let you come with me," Maria said. "I guess we must have suited Padre Diego's purposes."

"But Maria, why don't the friars allow us to go home? We've been here so long. You always said that Papa was one of the king's most trusted advisors. If that's true, why did he let the friars take us to Brazil?"

"We were kidnapped," Maria said, "taken by soldiers of the Inquisition. What could Papa do against them?" She lowered her voice again. "Don't forget that we were *conversos*. We were never truly safe." Maria picked off a piece of yellow straw sticking to Isobel's chemise. She broke off a little bit at a time, tossing the pieces away. "You know, just a few days before the soldiers came, I heard Mama and Papa planning something. I listened at the door and Papa said that we must all go to Amsterdam, where the Dutch government offered freedom. He said things were changing in Portugal and we could not stay any longer." She snapped the remaining end of the straw in half and clutched the pieces in her hand tightly. "I was so afraid when I heard him. I remember sneaking back to my room and covering my head with the pillows so they wouldn't hear me cry. I didn't understand and I didn't want to leave our home and our friends.

"I don't remember the soldiers coming, but I do remember loud voices and being put with you in a cart under a heavy blanket. You were crying." Isobel shivered. "You kept screaming for Mama," Maria said gently.

"We've been together ever since," Isobel said. "And we always will be together."

Maria pulled her sister closer, but was strangely quiet. Isobel felt only her sister's warmth and the soft straw under them.

"Do you remember being put on the ship?" Maria asked. "You were only six then, and you must have been confused." Isobel closed her eyes and tried to understand the images that clouded her mind. She thought she recalled the rolling of a ship and the sounds of crying, but her memories were unclear.

"We were forced onto a ship with many other children," Maria explained. "I recognized some of them. I tried to calm myself and make sure I didn't let go of you. I thought surely Papa would go to the king and tell him what had happened. Then the king would send word to the soldiers. 'The children of Abraham Ben Lazar are to be released!' But no messenger came. Only more children."

Isobel imagined the dim scene with children huddled together in a cramped room with open beams. Did she remember, or was she just creating a scene from Maria's words?

"Then I heard the sailors pull up the anchor." Maria was breathing fast now and Isobel felt a sweaty palm against her own hand. Maria spoke rapidly, as if she had to get the words out before they were lost. "The boat began to move and I suddenly realized that there was no one to depend on any more, only myself. Not Papa or Mama. And surely not the king." She stopped and took a deep breath. "I was only ten, Isobel. Younger than you are now." When she spoke again, there was sadness in her voice, as if she were choking back tears.

"I was a child when I stepped onto that boat. But I became a woman as soon as it sailed, for there was no more time to be a little girl. And I made a woman's vow that I would find Papa and Mama again, no matter how long it took. I'm going to keep that promise."

"How do you know we can find them in Amsterdam?" Isobel asked. She realized for the first time that her sister's plan was based on a guess.

"We can never go back to Portugal," Maria explained. "The Inquisition would only send us to another monastery. I'm sure Papa knew that. With both of us gone, I think he would have been more certain that he had to leave. And going to Amsterdam had been his idea all along. I am sure we will find them there. Then we will be free to be Jews again!"

Isobel closed her eyes and stroked Maria's back. She was afraid to tell her sister that she did not feel certain she was a Jew, although she could probably never be a Christian, either. The friars had made her hate their stern and shouted teachings.

"Now I have two more things that I want you to carry with you," Maria said. From her sack she withdrew a small Bible. "What the friars call the Old Testament," she began, "is also the Jewish Bible.

Whenever you are alone or afraid, just read the Bible. It will almost always have something comforting to say."

Isobel took the Bible and placed it carelessly in her sack. "If I am afraid," she protested, "I will come to you."

Maria reached for Isobel's hand. "There is one more part of the plan that I have not yet told you," she said slowly, and her voice quavered. "We must hide on different ships."

Isobel felt as though she had been struck by Padre Francisco's lash. The shock was so deep, so piercing, that she could not fully absorb her sister's words.

"You must have courage," she heard Maria say. "I've thought it over carefully, and I am convinced there is no way for both of us to hide on one small and crowded ship. It will be difficult enough if we are alone."

"No!" Isobel cried. "I won't leave you! I won't go alone!" What use would it be to go to Amsterdam if she had to leave her sister? "We've always stayed together. You're all I have!"

Maria held her close. "Do not be afraid, little sister. Don't forget that all the ships are bound for Amsterdam. It's almost like the oxen pulling two carts, one behind the other. It will only be a few weeks before we are together again."

Isobel had no good arguments, and she felt lost. Maria continued talking, refusing to dwell on the fact that Isobel would have to stow away alone.

"Look, Isobel, I have one more thing for you to take. Something special." Isobel squinted to see what Maria held in her hands. She thought she must be dreaming, for Maria held two beautiful silver hair combs! She reached out and touched the dainty, filigreed design. "They're for you, Isobel."

Maria pushed the combs into Isobel's thick hair, one at each side. Isobel could not see herself, but she felt beautiful. The combs were a treasure fit for a princess, and she was wearing them! "Where did they come from?"

"They are the last of my secrets. I was wearing them the night we were taken away. When we were put on the ship, we were all given frocks and needle and thread to take up the long hems. I managed to sew the combs into the seams of my chemise, and I have been able to keep them hidden in my clothes ever since. Tonight I'll sew them into your new chemise. They will be safe there."

She took the combs from Isobel's hair and slipped one in at each side seam. From the bottom of her own chemise, she produced a small needle with white thread, and set to work. "The combs are your treasure and your fortune. They are all we have in the world to remind us of home and family. Perhaps they will help you find our parents if we do become separated. But Isobel, if they become your only means of getting to Amsterdam, or staying safe, the combs can be sold. They are worth a good deal."

Isobel felt the loose hair where the combs had been. "I will keep them until I am home," she promised.

Maria kissed Isobel's cheek. "You are growing up, little sister, and you are stronger than you realize. I would not ask you to do this if there were any other way."

Isobel felt a mounting fear. She put her arms around Maria's waist and clung to her. "I can't go without you."

"You must," Maria said fervently. "This is our only chance." Isobel felt as if she were suffocating. Her breath came in short gasps. She wanted to escape from the friars and find her parents in Amsterdam. But not alone.

Maria stroke her back, gliding her palm across the crisp new chemise. "Go to sleep now, little sister, for we will need all our strength to get safely away from here. Close your eyes and dream of Amsterdam."

Isobel closed her eyes, but lay awake for hours, listening to the ceaseless chirping of crickets. She thought anxiously of Maria's plan and trembled in the darkness. Maria said she had become a woman when she sailed from Lisbon, she thought. Now I must do the same.

 # Desperate Escape

"Get up, you lazy girls!"

Padre Francisco's shouts were punctuated with a sharp kick aimed at Isobel's back. A searing pain shot up her spine as she struggled to her feet. She blinked into the semi-darkness of the barn.

What time was it? The chickens still roosted with their heads tucked under their wings, and even the crickets were silent. They were going to escape before the friars were awake. Padre Francisco had come too soon!

The priest strode toward the open door. "Get dressed and bring some water to Padre Pão. You are to do whatever he asks. When he has no more work for you, come directly to me."

Maria's shoulders slumped. "We have slept too late," she whispered. Isobel felt a knot tighten in her throat.

"We can't miss this voyage," Maria declared. A look of determination came over her. "We will have to get away in daylight. It is much more dangerous, but we have no choice."

The girls drew water from the well and turned toward the kitchen. "We don't know how much longer we have until the ships sail this morning," Maria said, worry showing in her voice. "There is no time to waste. We must make some excuse to go back to the barn without making Padre Pão suspicious."

"Bom dia," the cook greeted them. "I trust you slept comfortably." Isobel rubbed the sore on her back. "Come in," he said. "I have breakfast ready." He set three plates of food on the table, and Isobel's eyes widened. Each plate held two fried eggs, several pieces of crisp bacon, and two thick slices of bread spread generously with rich, creamy butter.

He sat down and beckoned the girls to join him as if they were invited guests. Isobel moved toward a chair, but Maria put a restraining hand on her shoulder.

"Thank you, padre, but we must feed the oxen first. And clean the stalls. Just a piece of bread to take with us will be enough." Isobel looked longingly at the food.

"The oxen can wait," the friar smiled. "While you are in my charge, I insist that you eat." The girls sat down obediently. Isobel sensed Maria's concern, but she was glad for the breakfast. It was only dawn. There must be time before the ships sailed. She would eat quickly. She savored the aroma of the food as Padre Pão recited a blessing.

"You will be here several weeks," he smiled as he ate, "and I may make you as plump and round as I am!" At the monastery the children were given only a piece of fruit for breakfast, or a slice of plain bread.

"I shall be fat in an hour!" Isobel blurted out, devouring a mouthful of eggs.

"We shall become good friends, you and I," Padre Pão said.

None of the friars had ever offered friendship before. Isobel felt guilty that she had to trick him into thinking all was well. She cleaned her plate and could not remember ever feeling so full or so satisfied. Maria stood up abruptly and removed her plate from the table. "We must look after the oxen," she said. Padre Pão looked with disappointment at Maria's plate.

"Don't you like the bacon?" he asked. "I sliced it myself."

Maria's face paled. "I'm sorry, Padre," she said. "I can't seem to develop a taste for it."

"I understand," he answered brusquely.

Isobel suddenly realized that Maria would be upset with her for forgetting the Jewish food laws and eating the meat of the pig, but she was not used to thinking of such matters, and her hunger had gotten the best of her. It was confusing to discover that Maria was angry with her for eating the bacon, and Padre Pão was disturbed because Maria had not eaten it.

Surely God would not intend one to starve, she argued with herself, but a voice within reminded her that with two eggs and buttered bread, she was not starving.

Isobel tried not to think about the bacon as Padre Pão asked the girls what tasks had been assigned to them for the day.

Maria's eyes darted to the window and Isobel looked outside. Fingers of light reached up over the horizon and the darkness had begun its retreat. "We are to report to Padre Francisco when you have no more work for us," Maria said dutifully.

The smile returned to the chubby friar's face and dimples creased his cheeks. "Then I shall not be done with you so quickly," he said. "You are good at finding the eggs the chickens hide in the barn, so spend some time gathering eggs." He winked at them. "Don't rush around or you might step on one. Do feed the oxen and then spend a while talking to them, for they are lonely, I think." He folded his hands across his stomach. "I should say you will be busy until lunch, yes?"

"Thank you, Padre," Maria said gratefully, and Isobel detected a sense of relief. "You are kind to us."

"Do not thank me for doing the Lord's bidding," he responded.

"Hurry up," Maria chided as she walked briskly to the barn.

"I can't walk any faster," Isobel complained. "My back hurts all the way down to my legs. There's a big lump where Padre Francisco kicked me."

Maria reached the barn first and dragged in a thick wooden plank that was used to bar the doors. Splinters of wood jutted menacingly from the edges where the casing had rubbed it raw. She had already pulled one side of the double door closed when Isobel entered.

"Help me," she said, as she struggled to fit the heavy board into place. Isobel bent down to lift one end of the plank, and cried out in pain.

"I cannot bend," she said.

"Perhaps God punishes you for eating bacon," Maria said, tugging at the plank.

"Maria!" Isobel protested. "I can't stand it when you sound like the friars. I'm sorry I ate the bacon! I didn't think."

Maria looked bewildered and let the beam drop to the floor with a thud. "I'm sorry," she apologized. "I shouldn't have scolded." She wiped her hands on her frock. "I guess I'm so nervous about getting away that I, too, did not stop to think." She put her arms around Isobel and kissed her sister's head. "Let me see your back."

"He's given you quite a blow," she said sympathetically as she examined the bruise. "There is a cut, I'm afraid, and it's swelling. Everything seems to be going wrong. Maybe we shouldn't even try." Maria looked searchingly at her sister. Her face was grim. "If the friars find us, our punishment will be harsh."

"I know," Isobel said. She straightened her shoulders and tried to look confident. "But we've got to try."

Maria struggled alone with the plank until the door was securely fastened from the inside. Then she retrieved their bags from the hay and handed Isobel hers.

"We must go now," Maria said. "Padre Pão said he did not expect us until noon, and with the door barred from the inside, it will take them some time to discover if we are really in here or not."

"But how will we get out?" Isobel asked, looking at the barred door. Maria pointed to the loft and a rickety wooden ladder leading to it. A small door at the top

opened to the outside of the barn, and a thick sisal
rope used for lifting hay bales hung from the rafters.

"If you think you can climb up, we'll slide down the
rope to the ground." Maria scrambled up the ladder
with her sack fastened to the cord around her waist.
The loft door creaked with disuse as she opened it and
pulled the rope until one end rested on the ground
below.

Isobel tied the sack as Maria had done, but paused
before ascending the ladder.

"I have an idea," she said mischievously. She stepped
to the oxen's stalls and unlatched the low doors that
penned them in. "You know how frightened Padre
Francisco is of the oxen," she said. "I wish I could see
his face when he gets the barn door open."

She climbed the ladder cautiously, bringing both
feet to rest on each rung before attempting the next.
"I'm all right," she assured Maria, as she saw her
sister's worried look. "I just have to go slowly." Maria
reached down and helped Isobel into the loft. The oxen
began to move about as they discovered that they were
no longer confined.

"Now, let's make sure they greet the good friar at
the door when he gets in," Isobel said. She began
throwing armfuls of hay toward the barn door and the
animals obligingly followed the trail until they were
contentedly feeding in front of it. "That should be a
proper welcome!" she said with satisfaction.

"We must not waste any more time," Maria cautioned. She grasped the rope and slipped down to the
ground.

Isobel felt a sinking feeling in the pit of her stomach.

"Don't look down," Maria advised. "Just watch the rope."

Isobel grasped the rope tightly, stepped off the ledge, and slid dizzyingly down until her feet hit hard earth. Pain coursed through her legs and back as she landed, but she kept silent and followed her sister into the thick bushes just beyond the barn. From her sack, Maria withdrew the collars and aprons she had made. "Let's put these on now," she said, "and hope we don't look too odd."

Isobel was filled with delight as she tied the long white apron around her waist. The girls helped each other tuck the hoods inside their frocks and replace them with the square white collars. Isobel smoothed her hair over her shoulders and thought of the silver combs hidden in her chemise. If only she could wear them, just this once. But she knew she must be patient.

"These hardly look like frocks any more," Isobel said, pleased with the effect. "I feel as though I'm truly wearing a new dress!"

"If we follow the road we came on, I think it will lead straight to the harbor," Maria said. "We should walk at a confident pace. Keep your head up and do not run," she cautioned. She took Isobel's hand in hers. "Then we must each board a different ship, and know in our hearts that we will be together again soon."

Isobel threw her arms around her sister. "I love you!"

"And I love you, too," Maria responded, hugging her tightly. "I believe that what we are doing is right and that God will protect us."

The girls walked just out of sight of the barn and church buildings. As they reached the front of the church, they heard the sound of a wagon's creaking wheels. They crouched behind a thicket and peered cautiously through the foliage.

Four friars alighted at the church steps, and Padre Francisco greeted them at the door, embracing each one in turn.

"*Bem-vindo!* Welcome!" she heard him say. "Leave the wagon, and I shall have the children attend to it."

"What children?" came the quizzical voice of one of the new friars.

"Why, we have brought two of the young *conversos* with us from the monastery. It will be good for them to see the Inquisition at work. Perhaps it will strengthen their beliefs when they see what happens to infidels!"

Isobel heard the friars laughing softly and the sound of the church door closing as the group disappeared inside.

"Quickly!" Maria urged. "They will start looking for us now. There is so little time! We must board the ships before they realize we have gone."

The girls began to move as fast as they could through the thick undergrowth, keeping their heads down to avoid being seen. Isobel's back and legs throbbed with pain the faster she went and she hoped the harbor was not far.

Behind her, she heard shouts and guessed that the friars had discovered the locked barn. Then she heard a dull, heavy banging. She looked questioningly at Maria.

"They're battering down the door," she said in alarm. "They know we're gone!"

Isobel gripped her sack tightly and pushed ahead. There was nothing to be said now. Both girls knew the seriousness of what they had done, and knew their punishment would be severe if they were caught.

Isobel tried to calm herself by imagining the expression on Padre Francisco's face when the oxen lumbered out of the barn. The battering and banging would frighten the animals, she knew, and they would surely charge forward as soon as the door gave way.

The two sisters approached the town's market area, where people bustled about despite the early hour. Women scrubbed the stone steps in front of their doors with stiff brown brushes, and peddlers filled baskets with their wares and hurried toward the waterfront.

Maria was out of breath, scanning the road and deciding which way to go. She stopped just before a row of shops and moved behind a tree. Isobel kept close to her side. A lanky boy stood not far from them, and a man approached him from a nearby doorway, carrying two large baskets filled with round loaves of bread. Isobel was close enough to smell them. The aroma reminded her of Padre Pão. She hoped the plump, round little Father Bread was not the one to open the barn doors.

"Ricardo," the man said, handing the baskets to the boy, "take these baskets down to the docks. The ships sail this morning, and there will be many who will buy one last bit of fresh food. And remember, the price is now a guilder for each loaf."

The boy began to protest, "But that is four times the usual price!"

"You must remind them that this is no longer a Dutch colony and their money is worth nothing. We must beg the Portuguese to accept it."

"Yes, Father," the boy conceded, "but they will be angry all the same."

"Perhaps, Ricardo," the father smiled cunningly, "but they will still buy. As soon as you have sold them all, hurry back, and I will have more loaves ready. Now, be off!"

The boy shuffled off, balancing the two large baskets on his shoulders. The path was clear now and Maria whispered to Isobel, "I think we should return to the road. We can travel to the docks faster if we are not held up by all these bushes and weeds." She paused and then said solemnly, "It is now that we must part. It will be harder for the priests to find us if we go our separate ways. They will be asking the townspeople if they have seen two girls, and if we are not traveling in a pair, it may protect us. I will go around the market-place that way," she said, pointing past the baker's house along the line of stalls. "I'm sure all paths lead to the harbor. You follow the way the baker's boy went. Just remember, don't run."

Isobel turned to Maria and saw that tears ran down her sister's face. She reached out to hug her, but Maria moved back, shaking her head. "No," she said, her voice breaking. "No goodbyes." She rushed toward the path, but then looked back and called softly, "Go with God, little sister. Go with God."

Suddenly Isobel was afraid. Her heart pounded in her

chest and she felt as if she could not breathe. She slumped down in the bushes along the roadside, unmindful of the prickly branches. She had not imagined what it would be like to escape alone and she felt unable to go on. She had wanted to escape, but that was when Maria was by her side.

Perhaps it would be better to simply wait to be caught, she thought. Maybe the harshest punishment Padre Francisco could give would not be as bad as trying to stow away alone on a strange ship. Her lips quivered and her eyes brimmed, but she forced herself not to give in to tears.

Maria is already gone, she reminded herself. To give up now would be never to see her or my parents again. It would mean going back to the monastery forever. Her mind was muddled in confusion.

Behind her Isobel heard men's voices talking in impatient tones. In the distance she saw several friars advancing on the narrow road, their sandals kicking up a haze of dust. The shock of seeing their approach moved her into action. I am the one who convinced Maria to go ahead with the plan, she thought. I wanted to escape. I can't let Padre Francisco catch me!

She pushed away the clinging branches and hurried along the road until she reached the open space at the edge of the dock. Peddlers shouted their wares in Portuguese and Dutch, and crowds of people waited to board the ships. Families stood close together amid piles of baggage and bedding. Behind her, the shouts she had heard in the distance grew louder.

"Runaways!" came the voices. "Look out for runaways!"

Isobel turned with the rest of the crowd and saw Padre Diego with a group of workers. She saw him gesture to his own frock, probably describing what the girls wore. Maria had been right about the aprons and collars. Soon it seemed that every voice buzzed with the message: "Runaways!" "Girls in frocks!" "Runaways!"

Isobel wanted to run to the ships and blend in with the passengers as they boarded, but she remembered Maria's caution and her injured back. If only Maria were with her! Everything would seem clearer and less frightening if her sister could tell her the right thing to do.

As she hurried toward the dock, looking behind her, Isobel was startled to bump into someone.

"Watch out there!" came a rough voice. Isobel froze. She would be caught, recognized! She looked at the person whose arm grasped hers. It was Ricardo, the gangly baker's boy, standing next to his baskets of bread halfway between the shops she had passed and the docks she must reach. "Look where you're going," he repeated with annoyance. "You nearly toppled my basket."

"*Desculpe.* I'm sorry," Isobel muttered and tried to pull away, but the boy hung on to her, looking her over carefully.

"You're a strange one," he commented, eyeing her dress and collar. Then a sudden burst of recognition came over him. "Why, you're . . . you're . . ."

"Let me go, Ricardo," Isobel said angrily, pulling her arm free. She saw two friars nearby and was afraid the baker's boy would give her away. "I wanted to buy a loaf of bread," she said, trying to sound dignified, "but I didn't realize I would have to deal with such a ruffian."

Ricardo's mouth dropped open. The strange child knew his name! He was thrown into confusion.

"Well, are you going to sell me a loaf of bread or not?" Isobel demanded.

"Yes, of course," the boy stammered. *"Desculpe,* I thought you were . . ."

"I am not at all what you thought." She bent down as if to examine the loaves of bread. Pain coursed up her spine and she felt dizzy and lightheaded. "Are these fresh?" she asked.

"Certainly. My father baked them only an hour ago. If you are traveling across the ocean, this will be your last fresh bread for many months. It is the best guilder you will ever spend."

"Guilder?" Isobel said with indignation. She remembered Ricardo's argument with his father. "A guilder should buy four loaves of bread! My mother sent me to make a purchase, not to be robbed."

"I know it sounds quite high," Ricardo said apologetically, "but the guilder is worth almost nothing now that the Dutch are leaving."

"To you it is worth nothing, but in Amsterdam it will be worth four loaves of bread," she said haughtily. "Keep your bread!"

She set her steps again toward the docks, her heart pounding inside her at the close call with the baker's boy, but with a sense of pride at her own quick thinking. I did that without anyone telling me what to say, she thought. Ricardo would never guess that I do not

even know what a guilder looks like! She was nearly
ready to congratulate herself, when she heard a voice
call, "Isobel!"

The distance to the throngs of people boarding the
ships was so close, yet seemed so far. Isobel began to
walk faster than her aching legs wanted to go. She was
nearly running, when a hand reached out and grabbed
her arm tightly.

Her heart seemed to stop beating as she turned. It
was Padre Pão who was holding her fast. His face
registered sadness and confusion as if his feelings had
been hurt.

"Isobel, come back to the church with me. I will not
let them punish you. You will be safe, I promise you."

"No!" Isobel answered. "Please, Padre, I beg you. Let
me go!" The fear and anxiety of the day became too
much for Isobel. Tears rushed to her eyes and spilled
down her cheeks, falling in big drops onto the apron at
her waist. Padre Pão looked pained, but he did not
loosen his grip.

Isobel slumped in despair. She raised her free hand
toward the friar and forced herself to look into his
eyes. In a barely audible voice she pleaded, "Please let
me go! I need my mother and father! In the name of
God, let me go!"

Padre Pão's head drooped and he looked as if he had
been struck. His hand fell from Isobel's arm and he
stepped back, shaking his white-fringed head. "I knew
we were wrong," he said softly, making the sign of the
cross. "God forgive us, we were wrong."

Isobel could not believe her ears. She thrust her bag
under her arm and rushed into the crowd of passengers,
never allowing herself to look back.

 # Hiding Place

Isobel pressed herself into the crowd of people that pushed forward onto the ship. A tall man jabbed his elbow into her shoulder, and a heavy-set woman holding a large bundle wrapped in patchwork stepped carelessly on her toes. She winced, but made no sound, hoping that no one would notice her. She glanced quickly at the people around her. What fine clothes they wore! How rich they looked!

How could I have thought I looked like these Dutch colonists in my drab, baggy frock and this makeshift apron? she worried. The other girls wore dresses of blue, green, or bright red, and their skirts were gathered full and trimmed in bands of satin ribbon. Their collars spread over low, square necklines and the fronts of their dresses were decorated with beautifully stitched designs. Where did they get such finery?

Even their aprons are stiff and pressed into sharp creases, Isobel observed, while mine is limp and wrinkled. Every foot she saw peeking out from beneath a swishing skirt wore either a sturdy wooden clog, or a dainty buckled shoe with a delicate, thin sole. She felt shabby and uncomfortable with her differentness, and she pulled at her frock in an attempt to cover her worn sandals.

Ahead of her, two husky sailors stood at the entrance to the ship. As the passengers surged on board, they directed them this way and that with hasty waves of their thick, burly arms.

Someone brushed against Isobel's frock, as if feeling its coarse fibers. She turned her head slightly to see a small boy, about seven or eight years of age. He stared at her with intense, sorrowful eyes. His hair was as pale as a turnip, and it fell below his ears. A small white cap, like others Isobel had seen today, sat upon his head. He wore short breeches and a jacket with long white streamers that hung from his shoulders and reached nearly to his waist. A slight, blonde woman, surely his mother, held fast to one of the long strips of fabric while balancing a large bundle of blankets and bags.

Isobel realized that she was observing the boy too closely. She turned her head away while the crowd of passengers pushed impatiently from behind, and concentrated on keeping her balance on the swaying plank that led to the deck of the ship. What if the child pointed her out to his mother? What if he alerted the sailors to the oddly dressed girl who stood beside him? But the boy remained strangely quiet, and Isobel could feel him staring at her without seeing his face.

As she approached the sailors, she felt an insistent

tug at her arm. She turned in alarm, certain that she was being pulled from the ship, but it was again the boy. He reached for her hand, slipped his small, soft fingers into her palm, and held tightly.

Just as one of the sailors eyed her directly, she was walking hand in hand with the child, who was, in turn, firmly in his mother's tow. The sailor motioned them brusquely toward the bow of the ship, mumbling something in Dutch.

Another obstacle! Isobel thought in horror. If anyone speaks to me, I won't understand them or be able to answer.

The boy dropped Isobel's hand once they were safely on board and was led away by his mother, who seemed to have taken no notice of her son's momentary companion. Isobel scanned the open deck, searching for a place to hide.

To her left, at the back of the ship, a two-tiered wooden structure rose up from the main deck. Bulky coiled ropes and knotted rigging seemed to fill every available space. Sailors made a steady parade up and down a narrow set of steps.

On the higher deck, a tall man dressed in a fine blue jacket and breeches, and wearing a broad-brimmed hat adorned with a large white plume, stood with his arms folded across his chest. His hat was set cockily at an angle, and dark, wavy hair fell below his ears to his clean-shaven chin, highlighting a bushy, drooping moustache.

As each sailor approached him, the man rocked back and forth on his heels and pensively stroked his moustache. Then, it seemed, a decision would be made, his arms would once again lock across his chest, and the sailor would hurry away.

That must be the ship's captain, Isobel decided. He is younger than I expected, but also sterner. I must stay away from the back of the ship if that is the captain's outpost. I have come too far to be discovered now.

A sailor carrying a large burlap sack over his shoulder shouted at Isobel in Dutch. When she did not obey his unintelligible order, he motioned her toward the bow of the ship with an impatient wave of his free hand.

Isobel knew that she had little time to hide before her presence came under closer scrutiny. Her eyes rested on a long wooden rowboat lying upside down and tied securely to the deck. Its high sides and narrow mid-section created an opening that looked like a dark, narrow cave.

Isobel gauged its size. It was long enough to seat a dozen people, she guessed, and perhaps high enough for her to sit beneath it. She could lie unnoticed in its darkness, yet enjoy a flow of fresh air through the opening created by its sloping mid-section.

Isobel walked alongside the inverted boat, stopping between it and the ship's rail. Fewer passengers and crew crowded the deck as people settled themselves below, and no one was near the longboat. She sat down on the deck, her back against the boat's curving polished sides, and measured its height against her head. It rose several inches above her. Carefully, she pushed her sack of belongings under the opening and glanced down. Even from her position so low on the deck, she

could no longer see the sack. She knew this might be
her only chance to hide before she was found, but still
she hesitated.

Then Isobel heard the sound of loud banter and
thudding footsteps. In one swift motion, she flattened
herself on the smooth planking and slid like a wet fish
under the dark coolness of the wooden boat. Maneu-
vering her feet into the narrow end with her head
facing the mid-section, Isobel blinked her eyes, trying
to adjust to the sudden dimness. She rested her head
on her hands and breathed with relief as the sailors
passed her by.

She could not believe how far she had come. She had
fooled the baker's boy, convinced Padre Pão to let her
go, and made it aboard the ship, and now she had
found a secure hiding place. And she had done all
these things without Maria. In just one morning, she
had accomplished more than she ever imagined possible.

The boat smelled of fish and salt, but she did not
find it unpleasant. It reminded her of her first exciting
glimpse of the harbor of Recife, and Isobel pictured the
bustle that was surely going on just a short distance
away at the water's edge.

I wonder if the friars are still searching for me? I
wonder what Padre Pão told them? Could he ever
admit he let me go, or would he lie to the others to
save me? Isobel imagined Padre Francisco's anger, and
her muscles stiffened. Her back throbbed with pain
where he had kicked her that morning. It was a reminder of Padre Francisco and her life at the monas-

tery that she would have to carry with her until it healed.

A hard object pressed into Isobel's side, and she reached down to see what was in her way. Immediately she realized that it was one of the silver combs sewed into the seam of her chemise. Her fingers lovingly caressed the outline of the delicate design. Soon she would wear the combs in her hair, and Maria and her parents would admire their beauty.

Her mind drifted and she felt lulled by the soothing sound of the waves as they lapped against the side of the ship. Her back did not matter anymore. Padre Francisco and Padre Diego did not have any meaning in her new life. Isobel was exhausted. She could not keep her eyes open, though she struggled to stay awake. In spite of her efforts, her eyelids closed and she fell into a deep and dream-filled sleep.

Isobel awoke to darkness and did not at first remember where she was. Cautiously she sat up, bumping her head on a wooden seat in the upside-down boat. She ran her hands along the deck until she located her burlap sack. Her head felt light, and her back sent slivers of pain in all directions.

The ship rode more heavily upon the water now, and Isobel knew that it was under sail. It seemed to rise up as if it would take to the air, pitch downward, and roll into the waves. Except for the sound of the planks creaking with each pitch and roll, an eerie stillness permeated the air.

Maybe I should try to stand at the railing and stretch my legs, Isobel thought. It might ease the pain in my back. Was it this morning that Padre Francisco kicked me? Or was it yesterday?

Isobel peered out and saw no one. Cautiously she slid from under the longboat and slowly stood beside it, holding the sack Maria had prepared. She was hungry, and she thought the lightness in her head was a reminder that she must eat to keep up her strength for the journey ahead. She withdrew one of the eggs and admired her sister's foresight.

The last time I ate was when Padre Pão cooked the eggs and bacon for breakfast, she remembered. At the same time she thought unhappily of her sister's displeasure when Isobel ate the forbidden meat. Oh, Maria, she thought silently, how can I tell you these laws mean nothing to me?

Isobel wondered if she had ever believed in anything—except Maria. She peeled off the eggshell and dropped the pieces noiselessly into the water. As she ate, she looked about her, adjusting to the pale moonlight that shone upon the full, billowing sails and outlined the ship in a ghostly halo.

The ship is beautiful, she thought. Stars blinked overhead. These are the very same stars that shine over the monastery in Bahia, but I am no longer the same girl who looks at them. For now I am free.

Isobel slipped back under the longboat that would be her home for many days, and a sense of peacefulness enveloped her. She closed her eyes and whispered quietly to the night air, "When we are together again, Maria, I will tell you how much I missed you."

 Shadows and
Whispers

"Catch her, Paulo!"

"Be quick! Grab her tail!"

Isobel opened her eyes with a start and saw a tangle
of children's feet scampering over the deck near the
longboat. She pulled back into the narrow end, tucking
the edges of her frock in close. It's morning, she
realized, and the children are playing on deck. I hope
this rowboat will not look as inviting to them as it did
to me.

"There she goes, Rachelle! After her!"

Suddenly Isobel was staring into the glistening eyes
of a black cat, which crouched under the opposite end
of the boat. The cat glared at her, as if Isobel were
intruding into its hiding place. A small hand reached
under the center of the longboat and groped about,
trying to find the cat. The frightened animal arched its
back and hissed a warning, and the small hand quickly
withdrew.

"Move over!" came a girl's commanding voice. "I'm not afraid of a harmless little cat."

To her dismay, Isobel saw a different hand appear under the boat, this one bigger and more aggressive. It waved around in wide arcs, expecting to find the cat, but to Isobel's horror, it grasped her burlap bag and pulled it into the sunlight of the deck.

Isobel barely stopped herself from crying out and grabbing the precious sack. She could not survive without food and water, and the slowly ripening bananas were to help her judge how many days had passed.

"Get away, Paulo! I found it, and that makes it mine! Maybe it's a treasure left by pirates. My father says the seas are infested with pirates and barely a ship escapes them. Perhaps a pirate hid his treasure here, planning to come back for it."

"Let's see!" The children clamored for a look and Isobel heard the sound of the sack's contents spilling out upon the planking.

"Eggs!" she heard the girl's voice announce in disappointment. "There's nothing here but eggs and bread and green bananas. Some treasure! And look, there's a small Bible. I guess this doesn't belong to pirates. Well, let's take it below deck, anyway. We can use some fresh food, instead of those awful dry biscuits."

There was the sound of scuffling and the rustling of fabric. "Stop, Paulo!" commanded the girl in an arrogant voice. "Look at him, everyone! He's hitting me! I think he expects me to put this back."

"Maybe we should leave it there," came a calm voice.

It sounded like an older boy. "We don't know whose it is, or why it was there. It might be important to someone."

"If anyone wanted it," came the girl's confident argument, "they wouldn't throw it under a smelly old rowboat." The voices trailed off. The children were gone, and Isobel's food was gone with them.

The cat sat back, licking its fur and eyeing Isobel haughtily. Then it walked proudly out from under the boat. Isobel twisted the corner of her apron nervously. How am I going to stay here without food or water? Oh, Maria, I know I should have kept the sack close to me. Isobel's disappointment in herself and her despair at losing the food were overwhelming. She wanted to cry and let out all the emotions that were choking her.

Instead she forced herself to think about what she should do. Really, she thought, it's no different than when Maria told me not to run on the docks in Recife. I must stay calm.

Isobel swallowed hard and the lump in her throat seemed to lessen. She chewed absently at her thumbnail. First, she thought, I must remember everything that was in the sack. She forced herself to make a mental list. Besides five eggs and bread and bananas, there was a small amount of dried beef, the para nuts that looked so much like Padre Pāo's fingers, and the bottle of water. That was probably the most important thing I lost. And, of course, there was the Bible. That was the least important thing, she decided, except that Maria had given it to her. She thought again of the water. Was there any way to replace it? She could last another couple of days without food, if she just had water.

Isobel tried to move into a more comfortable position. She sat up slowly. Her head felt hot and light and her legs cramped and tingly. The pain in her back had increased steadily since Padre Francisco had kicked her and now it took a great effort to move at all.

She listened to the harmonious sounds of a ship running smoothly. The thought that all was well outside her hiding place helped to calm her. She heard the sound of brushes rubbing across the deck and taut lines slapping rhythmically against the masts.

Tiredness overcame her. Her eyelids felt heavy and there was little to hold her attention and help her stay alert. Now she thought of the Bible that Maria had told her to read whenever she felt lonely. Why are you always right, Maria? she wondered. She knew now that even the book which she had so casually dismissed as unimportant would have been a welcome companion. As her head throbbed dizzily, Isobel lay down in her turtle-like shelter and tried to catch some of the breeze as it played coyly under the opening at the center of the longboat. Her eyes closed in spite of her wishes and she dozed fitfully.

Isobel did not know how much time had passed when she was awakened by three soft raps on the side of the boat. Had she imagined the sound? Everything around her seemed trapped in a dull haze. She listened intently and heard it again—three tentative knocks on the side nearest the ship's railing. She held herself still, but heard only the muffled noise of light footsteps retreating and the familiar sounds of creaking ropes, humming sails, and the slap of the ship as it cut into the waves. She put her face closer to the arched opening of the longboat and looked out cautiously. To her astonishment, she saw a piece of butter-yellow cheese and a small wooden cup only a few inches away.

Is this a trick? she wondered anxiously. If someone knows I am here, they could simply report it to the captain. They would not have to bait me like a mouse heading into a trap. It could be that someone has just left it there for a few moments and if I take it, they will become suspicious. Then I will set my own trap. But what about the knocking on my boat? I did not mistake that. Not twice.

The thought of the cheese consumed her, as her stomach twisted in hungry knots and her dry throat seemed to nearly constrict her breathing. Quickly she reached for the cup and then the cheese. She sipped gingerly at the water, finding the first few swallows painful to her parched throat. The cheese was moist and soft on her tongue, and it seemed the most delicious thing she had ever eaten. Isobel nibbled slowly, wondering if she should force herself to save some of it, but the piece was small, and her hunger too great.

When she had finished, Isobel set the empty cup back where it had been left and savored the lingering taste of the mellow cheese. Maybe you were right, Maria, and God is watching out for us. It seems someone wants me to survive. I hope you are safe. You would be proud of me for not crying when I lost the sack. I am trying to think carefully now so I won't do anything foolish.

The air grew cooler as the sunlight faded and the

breeze grew stiffer. Isobel lay on her stomach, resting her head on her arms and pushing her face closer to the opening. The ship pitched and rolled in a soothing rhythm. How can anyone complain about the motion of a ship, she wondered. I feel as if I am being rocked gently in a cradle. This time she willingly let herself fall back to sleep, for every limb and muscle felt weak, and the mere effort of keeping her eyes open was exhausting. Sleep also provided a release from pain and the increasing confinement of her hiding place.

As she slept, Isobel dreamed she was at the monastery again, listening from her bed as two friars conversed in the shadows outside her door. Maria, she whispered, why are they speaking Spanish? Do you think it is so that we will not understand them? A thick gray fog filled the room and obscured her vision until she could not see Maria, or her bed, or the two friars in the doorway, except for their feet. Isobel was surprised to notice that instead of their usual sandals, the two padres wore black leather boots. One pair was heavy and coarse, the other lighter, with thin soles and shining silver buckles.

Then Isobel awoke. Perspiration drenched her chemise, but she felt chilled and shivered all over. She heard voices. This wasn't a dream. Two men were conversing quietly in Spanish. The language was similar to her own Portuguese and she understood several words, but could not follow the entire conversation. One man seemed to give orders to another, and the second one protested.

"Silencio!" came a sharp reprimand. *"Es necessario."*

What is necessary? Isobel found herself wondering, and why are they speaking so softly? Her eyes kept closing and she was having difficulty concentrating on their words. Then came something about *"la carta."* Was he telling the man to change a map? Or change a chart?

"Sí, sí. Yo comprendo," came the second man's voice. I understand. He had a raspy voice and repeatedly cleared his throat. Now he coughed. *"Pero, yo quiero un demi del rescate."* Isobel understood that. It meant, I want half the ransom.

The first man argued back angrily, firing off a rapid stream of words. *"Tenémos una semana,"* he said finally. We have one week. Then came something about *"Cuba,"* and *"una carabela."* What was that? The words were hazy and unclear and their meaning escaped her.

Suddenly a word caught Isobel's attention. It was *"La Inquisición."* That was a word she would know in any language. Why were sailors on a Dutch ship talking about the Inquisition? Strong beams of moonlight lit the deck and reflected on the men's polished boots. As in her dream, the boots were all Isobel could see. One pair was indeed heavy black leather, like a sturdy work boot. These must belong to one of the sailors. But the second pair was different. They had thin soles and appeared to be made of fine soft leather. More to Isobel's surprise was the fact that atop each boot a filigreed buckle glimmered in the moonbeams. They looked like her precious silver combs. She blinked in disbelief, at the same time running her hands along the sides of her chemise. The familiar shapes met her grasp; her treasure was safe.

Not everyone on the ship is Dutch, she realized, and some are aware of the work of the Inquisition. Have the friars at the church offered a ransom to find me and turn me over to the religious courts? Perhaps they will put me on trial because I have run away from the monastery.

Isobel hugged her arms around her knees. She could no longer sleep, and she worried anxiously about the conversation she had tried to understand. What was going to happen in a week? What is Cuba? And what is *"la carabela"*? Isobel could not answer the questions, but her trembling now seemed to be more than the effects of her fever. Something was about to happen, and she had never before felt more lost and alone.

7

No Safe Hiding

The dawn came slowly, slipping under the longboat until it found Isobel shivering in the early morning dampness. She blinked her eyes open, but felt no comfort in the coming of day. By now she knew that a high fever gripped her body. She licked at her parched lips. With no prospect of water and no hope of improvement, she could only wait and try not to think about what she waited for.

A shrill whistle blasted two notes. There was a brief moment of silence; then the call was repeated. Isobel had learned that the whistle called the sailors on deck and that they took turns, some working or standing watch, others going below deck to rest. She listened to the familiar sound of boots hitting the planking, and the low gutteral greetings exchanged between the sailors.

As the men took up their jobs and the expected sounds met Isobel's ears, so too, did an unfamiliar one.

Someone walked lightly across the deck directly toward the longboat. The muffled footsteps drew near and then seemed to continue past it. Isobel hardly dared to breathe. Whoever had approached so stealthily must be standing just inches away. Had they come to spy on her? Then she heard three short raps on the outside of the boat. Her body tensed as she waited for the signal to be repeated, but instead Isobel heard the angry shout of a sailor stomping across the deck. His boots came to a halt on the side of the longboat opposite the railing. If someone has left food, she thought, he won't notice it unless he walks all the way around. To her relief, the sailor stood his ground, continuing his verbal assault on whoever it was who had just knocked on Isobel's hiding place. In a moment, she heard the softer footsteps move hurriedly away.

How strange, she thought, that my mysterious visitor did not answer the sailor. Perhaps he does not understand Dutch. Isobel waited until she was certain the sailor had also left before allowing herself to peer out from under her turtle-like shell. A slice of bread and another cup of water stood in the same spot as the last gift. She was convinced now that the cheese and water of the previous night had been meant to help her.

Still Isobel did not reach for the food immediately. Remembering her mental promise to Maria, she tried to be cautious. She waited and listened keenly for unusual noises. She pressed her palms against the deck and pulled herself closer to the opening. She winced at the tremendous pain in her back and a tingling numbness in her legs. The effort to drag herself just a few inches was draining. She closed her eyes and rested a moment, breathing in short, shallow breaths.

Listening for any sign of danger one last time, Isobel slowly extended her hand and brought the cup into her domain. Unable to wait another second, she lifted it to her mouth and drained its contents in just a few swallows. How dry her throat was! She dropped her head to her arm, disappointed that the water was gone so quickly. I cannot eat, she thought, but I must take the bread and save it.

Her hand fumbled toward the bread and, just as her fingers closed around it, a heavy boot came crashing down on her hand, pinning her fingers painfully to the deck.

"No!" she shrieked. Her voice echoed in the hollow wooden core of the rowboat, but was drowned in the husky, victorious shout of the sailor.

The sailor clamped his rough, callused hands around Isobel's arm and pulled her roughly from under the longboat, shouting loudly. Bright sunlight streamed into Isobel's eyes, making them blink and tear. She struggled to shade them, but the sailor pinned her arms behind her in a vise-like grip.

As her eyes began to focus, Isobel saw a crowd of faces. They laughed and stared and pointed at her. Where had they come from so suddenly? She looked around fearfully, expecting the Spanish sailors she had overheard to rush forward and take her away.

Then the crowd parted and silence fell. A tall, imposing man strode across the deck and stopped in front of Isobel and her gloating captor. Through the haze of her fever, Isobel recognized the rakish tilt of the man's white-plumed hat and the thick, drooping moustache that framed a firm, set mouth. It was the ship's captain himself.

His eyes narrowed and he folded his arms across his chest. He began rocking slowly on his heels, back and forth, back and forth, in a motion that made Isobel feel dizzy and nauseous.

The captain spoke, glaring at her fixedly, and Isobel was sure he was asking her a question, but she could not understand his Dutch. When she did not answer, the sailor gripping her arms yelled in her ear and twisted her arms more tightly behind her. He then directed his words to the captain, apparently giving an explanation of how he had found her.

I wonder if he will also tell how he tricked me and crushed my hand, she thought in defeat. He didn't have to hurt me. I would have come out.

The captain continued to rock back and forth and seemed to ignore the sailor. He had not once turned his gaze away from her and she could not bear to look at him directly. Again he seemed to ask a question. No one spoke.

Without warning, he unfolded his arms and Isobel tried to push herself back, afraid that he was going to strike her. But she only moved more closely against the sailor who held her. She was trapped between the two men. The captain, however, merely began stroking his moustache in a thoughtful manner.

"*Español?*" he asked. She shook her head no. "*Português?*"

"Sim! Sim!" Isobel answered now. "Yes! I speak Portuguese."

A man stepped forward from the crowd of people who watched with curiosity. He was dressed neatly in brown, with a white starched collar that hung across his shoulders. A plain black hat sat squarely on his head. He spoke in a simple and direct way.

"Desculpe," he said in clear Portuguese. He removed his hat momentarily and bowed curtly to the captain. "I speak both Portuguese and Dutch. I would be happy to interpret for you, if it would be of help."

The captain answered in halting Portuguese and then the conversation continued in Dutch. The captain now addressed the passenger in his native tongue and the man immediately related each question to Isobel in Portuguese. Isobel's answers went through the same process in reverse.

"I know that two young girls ran away from the friars in Recife, and that neither of them could be found before the ships sailed," the captain began. "You are one of those children, are you not?"

"Yes," Isobel admitted in a soft voice, looking down at her feet. Her head throbbed and her face felt hot. Still, the captain said that neither of the runaways had been found. There was hope that Maria had also boarded one of the ships and was safely hidden. At least the news was not that one of the girls had been caught!

"Is there another child with you on this ship?" the captain demanded.

Isobel could not have lied to this hard-jawed man

and she was glad she knew nothing of Maria's where-
abouts. "No," she answered firmly.

"You are a *converso?*" The interpreter asked Isobel
gently, but she had not missed the sharp tone in which
the captain had originally asked the question. How
should she answer? To be a *converso* was to secretly
follow the Jewish faith, yet pretend to be a Catholic.
She did neither. The captain repeated his question, but
the interpreter was silent.

"I am Isobel," she said finally, raising her eyes
briefly. Hearing her name, as if Maria was calling to
her, she straightened up and summoned all her
strength and pride. Her voice rose. "My name is Isobel
Ben Lazar."

"Well, Isobel," the captain continued, forgetting his
question, "why have you favored us with your presence
on our ship? Or should I say, under our longboat?"
There were titters from the crowd at his little joke.

Isobel stammered. "I . . . I must go to Amsterdam."

Now the captain seemed to be playing to the passengers and crew, who watched him appreciatively. "She
wants to go to Amsterdam. At least she is on the right
ship!" There was laughter then, and as the sounds of
the onlookers continued for a moment, the man who
was translating added two words of his own, quickly
and quietly. Isobel strained to catch them. He said,
"No more." He must mean I should say no more, she
thought, but why?

The man in the brown doublet now translated with
his own words. It seemed to Isobel as if he had taken
her side in the confrontation, and she felt an unex-
plained confidence in him.

The captain stroked his moustache impatiently. He began rocking on his heels, speaking decisively, as Isobel's unknown supporter explained.

"He is exasperated with you, child. He threatens to make you work on the ship and to have you returned to Recife as soon as we reach port."

"I am not afraid to work," Isobel offered. She lifted her head and searched the eyes of her interpreter. "But don't let him send me back!" she pleaded.

The two men carried on a brief conversation in Dutch and the captain's features registered an expression of surprise. He then smiled, but Isobel saw no warmth in it. He continued rocking and the board beneath his heels began to squeak. Isobel did not understand what was happening. They were talking about her, yet she was not a part of the discussion. All her life people had told her what to do. But she was here on this ship by her own efforts. It had been Maria's plan, but she had made it work. She could not let them make her go back to her old life at the monastery. Everything was different now, inside her.

The captain barked an order and the sailor released her arms. Isobel suddenly felt as if she were swaying on air. Her legs were weak, and as the ship rolled she wobbled unsteadily.

"It will be all right," her translator reassured her. "We are your friends and we will take care of you."

Isobel stared at the man in disbelief. "But who are you?" she asked him. "How can you be my friends when I don't know you? Why would you do this for me?"

The man smiled sympathetically. "We are God's

people, as you are, and that makes you a part of our family. We will not abandon you."

The man's words were kind, but she did not want to hear any more about God. What did he know about her? So many questions danced through her mind that she could not concentrate or search for answers.

The captain swayed rhythmically, back and forth, back and forth, his smile frozen in the space between them. Black spots danced before Isobel's eyes until she suddenly collapsed onto the cool wooden planks of the deck and darkness closed every image from her clouded eyes.

8

Below Deck

Muffled whispers reached Isobel's ears and played teasingly around them.

"Isobel! Isobel!" The whispers seemed to call her name, but she was too tired to listen and too tired to answer. Besides, she did not have to waste her energy trying to find out who called her. It was not Maria, because her sister was with her, picking flowers and braiding them carefully into Isobel's hair. Across the quiet fields Isobel saw an imposing stone castle. A trumpeter stood on a parapet and blew short, decisive notes. Isobel thought he must be announcing the arrival of her parents.

"Come, Maria, we must hurry. Give me the combs so they will know us." The trumpeter blew again upon his horn, more urgently this time, but Isobel could not find the combs. She felt along the seams of her chemise, but they were not there.

"Help me, Maria," she implored, but her sister stood

up, glided slowly toward the castle, and disappeared inside. Then Isobel remembered the shoes with gleaming silver buckles that had appeared just outside the longboat. The sailor took them, she thought. He stole my combs and used them on his dirty boots! My parents won't recognize me without the silver combs.

"Maria! Maria! I need you. Don't leave me!"

"I won't leave you," said a soft voice. "I am here."

Isobel's heart thumped wildly, and when she tried to call out, she could not speak. The flowers in the meadow blurred into a wild mix of colors that swirled before her eyes, making her head swim with dizziness. The meadow seemed to drop from under her feet, and Isobel felt herself falling. She screamed—a terrified, hopeless scream that echoed into the emptiness.

"Open your eyes, child. Wake up. It's all right."

Isobel's eyelids fluttered open, but her eyes would not focus. She saw a dim face, framed in dark, flowing hair, leaning over her. "Maria?" Isobel said softly. "Maria, is that you?"

She felt her head being cradled and a cup placed at her lips. "Here, child, drink this."

Isobel swallowed obediently and shuddered at the bitter disagreeable taste. Images came slowly into focus and she saw that the person who spoke was not her sister at all, but a woman whose face showed the beginnings of worry lines about the eyes and mouth, and whose rich, black hair was mixed with a few contrasting strands of gray.

"I do not think I am the Maria for whom you call," the woman said, wiping a cool cloth across Isobel's forehead. "But I am Maria, nonetheless. I am Maria

Levy, and I am relieved to see you awaken from your fever. The herbs I mixed have a bitter taste, but see how they have helped." A hint of pleasure turned into a small smile that curled around the corners of the woman's mouth. Isobel tried not to reveal her disappointment that this was not the Maria she had hoped to see.

"Where am I?" she asked. She was lying on a straw mat, wearing just a chemise. Bundles and trunks were piled against the wall, and pots and utensils were stacked neatly beside them. Isobel's eyes began to adjust to the dim light, and she discerned other figures nearby. Small groups of people were clustered in every available space. Some spoke Portuguese, and others spoke in the gutteral sounds of Dutch. The mixed din of conversation echoed about her.

"You are below deck on the Dutch ship, *The Valck*."

"How did I get here?" Isobel asked. "The last thing I remember is the captain telling me that I must work for my passage."

"You fainted on the deck. The captain carried on with a terrible bluster. We offered to care for you and he agreed right away. Abraham Israel, the man who translated, carried you down here."

"Was that this morning?" Isobel interrupted.

"No, child, that was two days ago. You have been burning with fever and unaware of anything."

Two days! Isobel was astonished. The sailors she had overheard talked about having only one week. She had already lost two days of finding a way to escape them. She closed her eyes for a moment, feeling her own weakness, and wondered if she was wrong about their intentions. If any of the sailors intended to turn her over to the court of the Inquisition, they would not have let Abraham Israel carry her below deck to be cared for. Perhaps they were not talking about her. But then who were they plotting against?

Maria Levy dipped a cloth into a pan of water and laid it gently on Isobel's forehead. Should she tell this Maria of the strange conversation? Perhaps she would understand its meaning. But Isobel had no reason to confide in her. And she understood so little of what she had heard, she did not think her story would make sense. She would keep her suspicions to herself until she knew for certain what the danger was.

As Isobel became more alert, she noticed the sleeve of the chemise she wore. It was intricately embroidered with yellow thread, barely noticeable against the white linen cloth. Isobel froze. Her fear of losing the silver combs threatened her again. She reached for the side seam to be sure she was not still dreaming, but there was no mistake. The combs were not there.

Maria Levy looked at her. "You must be wondering about the chemise. I dressed you in my daughter's clothes. Your back had a deep cut that was festering badly. I put a poultice on it, and already it is healing. I am convinced it was the source of your fever. Although there is very little water to spare, I washed your own chemise as best I could. Your clothes are here under your head."

Isobel's hands reached for the folded bundle and she quickly found the chemise. Yes, the combs were still sewn into the seams. She held the garment close to her chest as if she would never let it go. If she could feel the combs so easily, had Maria Levy also felt them when she washed it? But the woman said nothing, and Isobel decided her treasure was still safe.

"There is something else here that I think belongs to you," Maria said as she reached for Isobel's burlap sack. "I am ashamed that my daughter took it. We were disappointed that she would take anything that hadn't been given to her. When you were found, we felt certain it was yours."

"Yes, it is mine. There is just a small amount of food in it, which was to last while I was hiding." Isobel pushed herself up on one arm, trying to get up, but the dizziness returned. Maria Levy eased her back down onto the makeshift pillow. "I do not want to be a burden to you," she said. "Tell the captain that I am ready to work. I am not afraid to work, Senhora Levy."

"Just call me Maria. We are not very formal here." She brushed Isobel's hair off her forehead. "There is always time for work, child, so do not rush to it. You still need rest and quiet. Close your eyes now and sleep. When you awaken you will be more ready to deal with things."

The woman's words were comforting, and Isobel felt the tension in her body easing. She awoke several hours later, restored and clearly aware of what was going on around her. She remained still for a while to listen to the animated conversations of the families clustered together in the crowded hold.

"There will be no schooling for a while, Davi. You'll help me set up a butcher shop in Amsterdam."

"But I don't want to be a butcher," a voice protested. "I'm going to be an artist."

"You'll be a butcher first if you ever want to study drawing," the first man chuckled. "Artists earn about as much as Torah scholars."

Laughter rippled across the group. Then the first man spoke again. "If only I could marry off Rachelle. But she's so spoiled, who would take her?" More laughter followed as a young girl's voice protested sharply. "I have no intention of marrying anyone unless I choose him myself!"

"How about letting Rachelle live with me when we get to Amsterdam, Asser? I can sell fancy needlework, but I'll need help with the baby. And in the evenings Rachelle can practice her sewing. She's got a talent for it."

Isobel heard how easily the men and women talked with each other. Even the children were included. How different from Isobel's own experience, where children were isolated from adults. Nor had she ever seen so many women in such familiar and comfortable association with men.

The only women she had observed were the few natives who brought fruit to the monastery in Bahia. They hung back near the kitchen door, never saying a word, while the friars chose fruit from their baskets. They never asked for money, but simply accepted the coins the friars offered, tucked them into their bright headscarves, and backed away.

"Oh, look!" announced one of the young girls in the group. "Isobel's awake!" Isobel's cheeks flushed with embarrassment as she became the focus of attention. She was relieved to see Maria Levy step over to her side.

"Are you feeling better, child?"

Isobel nodded. "I think I might be able to get up now," she said quietly. "I really must find the captain and arrange my passage."

"Not just yet," Maria cautioned. "I am afraid the cut on your back will be aggravated if you move around. Here, I'll prop you up, and perhaps you can drink some broth."

The people returned to their own conversations while Maria tended to her young patient. Isobel freshened her face and hands with a wet cloth and vigorously brushed her tousled hair to a silky luster. She would never keep her long hair hidden beneath her clothes again.

"Muito bem!" Maria concluded. "Very good! Now you are ready!" She served Isobel a small wooden bowl filled with tasty broth, and as she sipped the hot soup, Isobel looked around her. The space below deck was small and crowded, and passengers seemed to cluster together in family groups. The air was heavy with unfamiliar smells steaming from different cook pots. Isobel saw one man say a blessing over his family's meal as each of them bowed their heads and dutifully made the sign of the cross before taking up their plates.

Maria pointed to the man who had served as Isobel's translator. "There is a face you may recognize," she said. "May I present Abraham Israel de Piza, his wife, Gloria, and their sons, Franco and Avram. Abraham is a maker of berimbaos, and a scholar of Torah."

Isobel could barely believe the casual way in which the Torah was mentioned. She knew it was a scroll of the Jewish Bible, but the word was forbidden in the monastery and was rarely whispered among the children. Now she knew that the families who had so readily come to her assistance were Jews, and yet they seemed unafraid to express their beliefs. If they had helped her because they thought she was one of them, that was more reason to be on her own as soon as possible.

Abraham smiled the same sad, sympathetic smile that Isobel had seen before. "Correction," he said. "I am a scholar of Torah first and a maker of musical instruments second."

Isobel did not know what kind of musical instrument a berimbao was, but her quizzical look was answered when Abraham and his sons, both already young men, took small brass instruments from their pockets and placed them to their lips. The metal instruments were shaped like horseshoes with a thin brass strip extending from the open end. They plucked at the protruding piece and breathed through the rounded end, and to Isobel's delight, a soft sweet sound filled the air. Then, before Isobel could thank them for the music or for Abraham's help, the family rejoined the group seated on the floor.

Other Jewish families traveling from Recife were introduced to Isobel, and she sensed the close spirit that bound them together. There was David Israel Faro, an exporter who, with his wife, Matilde, and their four children, hoped to start a new business in Amsterdam. There was Mose Lumbrusco, his chubby wife Sultana, and their son and daughter. Mose explained that he had lost his profitable sugar plantation in Recife, but with the help of relatives, hoped to find a new beginning in Amsterdam. Next came a tall, slender woman who looked joyfully at her gurgling baby.

"This is Judica Mereda," Maria said. The child's arms waved energetically, trying to pull her mother's loose brown hair. "Her daughter's name is Rayna."

Isobel's glance fell on the boy she had observed while boarding. He looked at her with familiarity, it seemed, and Isobel tried to decipher the message in his pale blue eyes. "That is little Paulo," Maria said of the child. "He is eight years old this week, aren't you, Paulo? And this is his mother, Rachel Nuñes."

Isobel took the opportunity to speak to the boy. "I met you when I came onto the ship, Paulo. You helped me get past the sailors by holding my hand as if I were part of your family. How did you know I needed help?"

The child looked at Isobel with such concentration that she felt his eyes piercing hers, but he did not answer. His mother spoke instead, in a pained, quiet voice. "He cannot talk," she said apologetically. "I'm sure he is pleased that he was of help."

Paulo stepped forward and took something from under his loose doublet and held it out to Isobel. It was a small wooden cup, and Isobel recognized it immediately. Here was the child who had brought her cheese and bread and water when she had given up hope. He had known that she was hiding under the rowboat. Two things became clear to her: he was the youngster who had tried to keep the other children from taking her sack of food, and he was the one spotted by the sailor just before she was caught. He had not answered the sailor's shouts because he could not speak.

"It's not your fault that the sailor caught me," she

said, anticipating his guilt. She reached out and rested her fingers lightly on his arm. "The food and water saved me, and so did being discovered." Paulo did not smile, but he placed the cup in Isobel's lap, gesturing to her with his finger.

"Is this for me?" she asked, and he nodded slowly. "Thank you, Paulo." What a sad child, she thought. I must find a way to repay him for helping me.

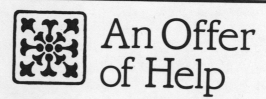 # An Offer of Help

Maria Levy beckoned to a young girl. "Isobel, this is my daughter, Rachelle." Isobel knew she ought to smile at the girl, but she was irritated that Rachelle had taken her sack. The girl had her mother's dark complexion and long, black hair, but Isobel did not see the same kindness. Rachelle regarded Isobel coldly and said nothing.

"You should apologize for taking her sack," said an older boy. "It was very wrong of you." He was olive-skinned like Rachelle, but tall and slender like the saplings that seemed to shoot up overnight in the forest after a tropical rain.

"Don't tell me what to do, Davi!" came Rachelle's imperious answer. "There is nothing to apologize for, because I did nothing wrong. How was I to know a dirty burlap bag filled with eggs and bananas belonged to someone hiding under a rowboat?"

"Rachelle! Children! Please!" Maria interrupted the

argument immediately. "I am ashamed of you, Rachelle. I realize that you did not stop to think that the sack belonged to someone who needed it. But must I apologize for your rudeness as well as for your thoughtless actions?"

Isobel was sure she had never seen a child so outspoken and brazen. At the monastery, she would have been whipped soundly for her lack of respect. Yet Rachelle did not seem at all ashamed of her behavior. She gave a deep curtsy to Isobel, dropped her head low, and said mockingly, "I humbly beg your forgiveness for any inconvenience I may have caused."

"That will be quite enough," said Maria reprovingly, but the girl continued.

"Just because Davi's fifteen, he thinks he knows more than anyone!" she railed. "Why don't you tell him to apologize for telling me what to do!"

Maria looked embarrassed. "Such children!" she said, and the others chuckled uncomfortably.

"And I am the father of such children," said a deep voice. A tall, well-groomed man stepped forward, stooping under the low beams of the lower deck. His large brown eyes gazed intently at his children. Silence fell over Rachelle and Davi although he had not said a word to them. He turned to Isobel.

"I am Asser Levy. Like my friend, Abraham Israel, I am a perpetual student of Torah, but since one makes very little money studying God's word, I am also a humble butcher by trade."

There was more appreciative laughter and someone commented, "As long as he doesn't butcher his readings of Torah, we are all right!"

Asser smiled at the joke, but as he seated himself on a large barrel, his face grew serious. His long legs were sprawled out in front of him and his clasped hands dangled between them. "You must be wondering who we are," he said. "Do you know anything about the colony at Recife?"

Isobel shifted on her mat and looked down at the patchwork coverlet spread across her legs. "I know there were Jews living there and that they had to leave when the Portuguese came," she said. She remembered how the friars had complained that General Barreto should have been harsher with the defeated colonists. Now that she had met the people whose lives were affected by his orders, she was relieved that he had spared them.

"Originally we came from Portugal and Spain," Asser explained. "A Dutch colony was a safe home for us. The courts of the Inquisition could not reach us there. Some of us have lived in Recife for thirty years, others for a shorter time, but it was our home."

Mose Lumbrusco had a round, jowly face and he spoke in a deep voice, sighing between breaths. "When the Portuguese attacked, we fought hard alongside the Dutch to repel them. Some of our community, like the husbands of Rachel Nuñes and Judica Mereda, gave their lives in the struggle. But still we could not overpower them."

"Now we are wanderers again," said his wife, her forehead creased in a deep frown. "We had to sell everything. Our homes, our businesses. Mose had to sell our sugar plantation for half its value." She spread her hands in the air and shrugged. "What else could we do?"

Asser slid his legs forward, bumping against a pile of bedding. He raised his hands toward the beams above him and nodded his head. "Still, by God's grace, we are together and we shall care for each other." He looked at Isobel again. "Now that you have escaped from the monastery and are alone in the world, we invite you to join us."

"And we can offer to pay for your passage," said Abraham. "We have an emergency fund to help those of us who are in need."

Isobel searched for the right words to say. It seemed everyone awaited her response and she was uncomfortable with so much attention. "I am alone on this ship," she faltered, "but I am not alone in the world. My sister and I lived at the monastery for six years after the Inquisition's soldiers took us from our parents in Lisbon. If I can just get to Amsterdam, I know I'll find them there." Isobel was careful not to mention Maria's name or to reveal where her sister was. She still feared the unknown plans of the two sailors she had overheard. She thought of asking Asser about the disturbing conversation, but there were so many passengers in the crowded quarters, and she had no way of knowing who might be unfriendly.

"There is no need for you to tell us more, child," said Maria Levy. "We know all that is necessary, which is that you need help on your journey. In return, you need only know that we are here."

Asser moved to the back of the group and the other men and older boys followed. They were soon engrossed in a lively discussion, their hands waving excitedly in the air as each strove to make his point. Mothers led the younger children off to their designated sleeping spots, straw mats were rolled out, and Isobel watched longingly as the sleepy youngsters were tucked under light blankets and kissed goodnight.

Rachelle marched past Isobel with her chin in the air. She rolled out her mat as far from the newcomer as she could. Isobel pushed the trunk that had supported her out of the way, and lowered herself onto her pallet. After her long sleep during the day, she felt restless and lay awake listening to the talk around her and the sounds of creaking planks overhead. There were no stars to watch down here and no breeze to stir the air.

From the corner of her eye she saw Rachelle unlace the front of her satin dress and pull it over her head. Isobel could not help noticing the girl's linen chemise. It had deep embroidered cuffs at the wrist, and a hem trimmed with a scalloped border. Rachelle dropped her dress carelessly beside her. Then she pointedly turned her back to Isobel and went to sleep.

She doesn't deserve such fine clothes! Still, Maria, she thought, although everyone here isn't perfect, I am being well cared for. And I won't have to put up with Rachelle much longer. Aren't you proud of me for making it this far? If only I knew that you were safe.

Isobel was still awake when everyone else had gone to sleep. She could hear the slap of the sails only faintly and was aware of the restless movements and mingled breathing of the passengers.

She pulled off the soft chemise in which Maria Levy

had dressed her and replaced it with the one that held her precious combs. She folded the borrowed garment neatly and placed it under her frock. Her fingers stroked the flawless fabric one last time as she put it aside. I do regret having to part with such a fine chemise, she thought, but I cannot sew in my combs or I might be discovered. And I would much rather be wearing something that you made for me, Maria.

She was relieved to again feel the silver combs close to her body. She settled back and listened to the sounds which surrounded her. Baby Rayna fussed in her sleep and then quieted as Judica gently patted her. Several men snored in different corners of the cramped space, their separate rhythms conflicting with each other. Isobel's room at the monastery had been crowded with pallets as well. How many times did I wake up in the night and feel comforted by the soft, steady breathing of the others? She felt a longing for the friends she had left behind. We had no time for playing selfish games, like Rachelle. We needed each other.

But I can't let myself become dependent on these families, she decided. They are kind, it's true, but I will be leaving them in just a few short weeks. How strange that they were unafraid to come to my aid while the other passengers were content to laugh at me. They seem certain they are in no danger. I hope they are right.

But I must think of my own way to keep the captain from sending me back to Recife. I told Asser I was not afraid to work. If I do a good job, perhaps the captain will be more sympathetic. If the sailors try to turn me over to the judges of the Inquisition, I will throw myself on his mercy. And if I work for my passage to Amsterdam, I will have a strong argument against him sending me back to Recife.

Yes, she thought with resolution, that is the answer. Tomorrow I go to work for the captain of *The Valck*. Isobel turned uncomfortably on her mat. The journey to Amsterdam is so long, and I have only just begun. And I miss you, Maria.

 # Winds of Suspicion

"Please, Maria, may I go up on deck and meet with the captain today? Really, I feel quite strong." Isobel looked appreciatively into the woman's face, feeling a closeness that she couldn't quite explain and did not wish to acknowledge. True, Maria Levy had cared for her, and the woman's medicines had cured her, but she had known her only a short time and would not have the chance to know her well. As soon as the ship reached Amsterdam, she would probably never see her or any of the others here again.

"Well, child, I think you'll have to be careful and not overtire yourself. Don't forget you have not yet tried to keep your balance on this swaying ship. I don't want you to fall and hurt yourself again."

Maria put a protective hand under Isobel's arm and helped her stand. She wobbled a bit unsteadily, but soon felt the ship's rhythm and adjusted to it.

"I don't suppose you plan to meet the captain in

your chemise?" she smiled. Isobel bent down slowly to retrieve her dusty brown frock. It was wrinkled from having served as a pillow, and she felt ashamed to have to dress so shabbily.

"I think a ladylike appearance in front of the captain will help form his good opinion of you," said Maria as she looked purposefully through a small trunk. "If you stand before him in your friar's robe, you will only remind him of your escape from the monastery." Isobel admired the woman's wisdom. She had not considered the effect of the frock.

"Ah, here it is," Maria announced, pulling a rustling mass of sky-blue fabric from the trunk and shaking it out. "This is Rachelle's dress, and I think it's exactly the right size for you."

Isobel was nearly speechless. The color of the gown reminded her of the sparkling ocean at Recife. The neckline was low and square, the flowing sleeves reached all the way to the skirt's hem, and the bodice and skirt border were trimmed with deep blue braid. Isobel took a breath. "Do you think it might fit me? It looks so big!"

Maria laughed, seeming to enjoy Isobel's delight and her lack of perception of her own stature. "You are simply not used to the full cut of the skirt," she assured her. "You're growing into quite a tall young woman."

Isobel looked down at herself. Was she really getting tall? She reached for the dress, so overcome with excitement that her fingers trembled. The cloth felt silky and elegant as it slid against her skin.

"It needs a stomacher," Maria said, reaching into the

trunk and producing a hard, wedge-shaped object covered in white linen with birds and flowers delicately embroidered on it. "This fits into the bodice." She laced the stomacher into place and fastened the hooks at the front.

"It's perfect!" Maria announced. She brushed Isobel's hair and added a tiny lace cap at the back of her head. Isobel insisted on wearing the collar and apron that her sister had made, not wishing to borrow any more of Rachelle's clothes. She wondered if the selfish girl had been consulted about the dress, but her excitement overcame her concern. She felt positively elegant as she swished the skirt with her hands. Her fingers tingled against the slippery sheen, and she reveled in its luxurious sound. She almost reached out to hug Maria, but held back at the last moment.

"Thank you," she said. "I will be very careful of the dress and return it after I meet the captain."

"Rachelle has many dresses," Maria sighed. "She will certainly not miss this one. It's a welcoming gift for you." She smiled at Isobel and said, "If you wish to see the captain, you should go immediately before he becomes too busy. Let's see if Abraham is free to accompany you, as you still need a translator. There is much for us to do today because it's Friday and we are preparing for the Sabbath."

In a moment, Abraham was leading the way up to the deck and Isobel was following nervously behind. Surely, she thought, the captain will not put me in prison or send me back to the monastery. Not when I look like this!

"*Bom dia!*" called a cheerful voice. Isobel looked up

to see Davi smiling broadly. He had the same large, dark eyes as his father, but his gaze was not at all serious.

"So! The little friar is transformed into a princess! Your servant, Your Grace!" He bowed low, doffing his hat in a sweeping gesture. Isobel felt her face flush hot with embarrassment. How could Davi have guessed that she felt just like a princess in the new dress? She hurried after Abraham and looked back only to see Davi grinning after her.

Of course, Isobel thought, he's only teasing me. I may feel like a princess, but no one would truly think I look like one. Maria would scold me for such silliness!

There was no sunshine to greet her when they reached the deck, but a strong breeze rustled Isobel's skirt and blew at her hair. The sails looked like fat flour sacks as the wind puffed them full. She took a deep breath, relishing the clean salt air. She turned her head toward the water, and a surprising sight met her eyes.

"Abraham!" she called, reaching for his arm to stop his quick progress. "Look at all the ships!"

Abraham smiled. "There are sixteen ships, all bound for Amsterdam. We left Recife together because it's safer. It discourages pirates, and allows the captains to help each other if difficulties arise."

A deep sense of longing overcame Isobel as she watched the ships glide toward the horizon. She was certain one of those ships carried her sister. But which one? Each vessel seemed so close, yet so unapproachable.

"Is your sister on one of those ships?" Abraham guessed.

"It's my older sister, Maria," she blurted out, unable to keep her feelings to herself any longer. She blinked back tears. "She planned it this way because she didn't think we could both hide on one ship. I didn't want to go alone . . . to leave her . . . but she said I had to, that there was no other way. I don't even know if she's safe." She leaned against the railing, watching the waves crash against the bow.

"You must be optimistic, child. Your sister was wise to separate from you. Not only is it harder to hide two people on these crowded ships, but a captain is much less likely to tolerate two stowaways than one. Each of those vessels carries a group of Jews leaving Recife just as we are, and your sister is sure to find sympathy no matter which one she is on." He patted Isobel comfortingly. "It will not be many more weeks before you and your sister are reunited in Amsterdam. Come now, let's see if we can settle your passage."

"Yes," Isobel agreed, turning away from the railing. She prayed Maria had found as much kindness as she had. "There is something I wish to tell you, Abraham, before we get to the captain. The offer to pay my fare is a generous one, but I have decided that I wish to work for my passage. It will make me feel useful and I hope it will keep the captain from sending me back to Recife."

Abraham bowed with the same short motion she had seen when he introduced himself to the captain. "I respect your wishes," he smiled. He turned and proceeded on to the captain's position at the rear of the ship.

Isobel walked stiffly in the new dress, unused to the rolling ship and the billowing skirt. She climbed the steep stairs to the captain's perch, tightly gripping the ropes that served as a makeshift banister. Standing in front of the captain once again, Isobel smoothed down the ruffled fabric and tried to calm herself.

The captain seemed so tall and imposing with his cocky plumed hat and his habit of rocking impatiently on his heels. Isobel felt a tightening in her throat.

I'm not going to let him scare me the way the friars always did, she determined. She forced herself to look the man squarely in the face, as she had seen her sister do when confronted with Padre Francisco.

"Bom dia!" the captain said solemnly in his accented Portuguese. "I see the little stowaway is feeling better. What shall I do with her?"

"She wishes to earn her passage to Amsterdam," Abraham explained.

The captain began rocking back and forth on his heels and returned to his native language, as if to shut Isobel out of the discussion. But as Abraham translated, she looked at the captain unflinchingly.

As the conversation progressed, Abraham reported that Isobel would be allowed to work for her passage, and if her job was done to satisfaction, she would not be forced to return to Recife. With that battle won, Isobel felt more confident.

"Can I work directly for the captain?" she asked. "I have a neat script and I could copy documents or write his letters." The captain laughed with amusement.

"He points out that you do not speak Dutch," Abraham explained.

"I could clean his cabin, then. I'd do a good job!" But the captain wanted no part of her.

"He says you're to work in the cook room, Isobel. The cook speaks Portuguese and you'll be out of the captain's way." Abruptly, the captain dismissed them with an impatient wave of his hand.

"There is no arguing, Isobel," Abraham consoled her as they left the quarter deck. "At least you have received a pardon for hiding yourself on the ship. I didn't think the captain would reverse his decision to send you back so easily."

In the short time since she had first come up from the passengers' quarters, Isobel felt a change in the wind. From the refreshing breeze that had first met her, she now felt a less controlled wind, which seemed to shift about from several directions and which was heavy with moisture. Her hair blew across her face and then behind her, swirling into tangles. The waves were higher and the ship rolled more sharply. Isobel reached out and held onto the rigging to steady herself as she stumbled forward, trying to keep up with Abraham, who walked steadily ahead of her. Her wide skirt caught on a wooden handle protruding from a mast, and as Isobel tugged it free she thought that her old frock did have some good points. At least it stayed close to her.

They stopped at a small kitchen tucked under the front deck. It had thick wooden walls and a strange gate-like door. The top half was open wide and the lower half fastened shut. "What kind of a door is this?" Isobel asked.

A swarthy, bearded man stepped up to the opening and answered Isobel's question in perfect Portuguese. "This crazy door is one of the most useful inventions on this entire ratty ship," he thundered. "When I leave the cook room unattended, I fasten both pieces closed. When I'm here working, I keep the top half open so I can get a breath of air and the bottom locked tight to keep out those thieving, hungry sailors!" The man burst into a loud, bellowing laugh and smiled broadly to expose several missing front teeth. "You here inspecting the door, or do you have business with me?" Abraham introduced himself and Isobel and explained that the child was to help him with his duties. "There's no space in this mouse-sized room for another man, but perhaps a pint-size girl might be a perfect fit." He leaned forward and eyed Isobel critically. "Can you handle a paring knife, child?"

"Yes, sir!" Isobel answered confidently.

"Sir, is it? If she calls me 'sir,' she's hired!" the man said to Abraham, and he unlatched the bottom portion of the door and ushered Isobel into his tiny work space. Abraham wished Isobel well and headed back below deck, apparently confident that she was in good company.

"Actually," the talkative cook said, "everyone calls me '*Pescador*, the fisherman.' They say I look like a fish, smell like a fish, and know how to cook fish in a hundred different ways. Actually, they're wrong. I may look like one and smell like one, but I can cook fish in a thousand different ways. Anyway, child, just call me

'Cado' for short, and I'll call you 'Izzy,' if you don't mind. I don't like wasting time."

"Yes, Senhor Cado, sir, that's fine. If you'll just show me the paring knife, I'll get right to work."

"That's the spirit, Izzy," the cook said cheerfully. "There's a pile of potatoes that need skinning, because if supper isn't served on time here, there's sure to be fire and brimstone raining down on old Cado."

Isobel walked over to a basket of potatoes with a small paring knife sticking out of one of them. A three-legged stool stood next to it, and Isobel sat down and started work. She began to relax. Her meeting with the captain was over and she was assured of her passage to Amsterdam. For the first time since she had run away, she knew exactly what to do. Right now, she did not have to think about anything, for potatoes made no demands. They merely waited to be peeled.

"Why, you're an absolute natural," Cado praised her, "or else you've had a lot of experience. Where do you come from, child?"

Isobel ignored the question and asked one of the cook instead. "I thought this ship was Dutch. How come you speak Portuguese?"

"I speak everything. I've been on so many ships and laid over in so many ports, and worked with so many different men, I'd never last if I didn't. I'm a native Brazilian, myself. Spoke Portuguese when they were in charge, then learned Dutch when they took over. I also speak Spanish, French, English, and a smattering of Tahiti dialect, too!"

Isobel remembered the conversation she had overheard under the rowboat, and her old fears returned.

What if Cado was one of the sailors she heard speaking Spanish? She looked to see if his boots matched the ones she had seen, but Cado was barefooted. That didn't mean he never wore boots, though. She tried to make her voice sound casual. "Are you the only sailor on this ship who speaks Portuguese?"

"There's a few others for me to converse with. A few Spaniards and a few Portuguese, too. Why, the first mate's a Spaniard and so's the helmsman. It's an international crew, I'd say."

Isobel turned a misshapen potato over in her hand while she thought about that piece of news. Working in the cook room might turn out to do more than just earn my passage to Amsterdam, she thought. Cado might even understand the plan I overheard. Maybe I can trust him with the story when I know him better. He doesn't seem like the type of man who would be part of the Inquisition.

"Where did you say you came from, child?" Cado repeated. Isobel hesitated. Perhaps she should test him with a bit of information that could not hurt her further.

"I'm the stowaway," she admitted. "That's why I'm here working with you. To pay my passage."

Cado raised one eyebrow and looked at Isobel quizzically. "You say you're the clever one who managed to hide out on this ship? You sure don't look like a stowaway. You know, that's a pretty fancy suit of clothes for a cook room."

"You're right about that," Isobel agreed. She wiped her hands on her apron and pushed the skirt protectively closer. "This outfit was just borrowed to impress the captain. The only other thing I have to wear is an old friar's frock, hood and all."

Cado's eyes bulged in disbelief. "Don't tell me you're one of those poor children they've got working at the monastery in Bahia? Why, those youngsters are treated like slaves, plain old slaves. I've seen them myself and heard plenty of horror stories to boot. If you managed to escape from that fortress, you have my admiration, Izzy."

Isobel smiled with relief. She had judged the cook well. She was certain now that he did not believe in the horrors of the Inquisition and thought she could trust him if she had to. She had never realized that so many people knew of the children at the monastery. But she had never known anyone outside the monastery until now.

The wind picked up, and by the time Isobel had peeled and cut all the potatoes, the boat was pitching mightily as it crashed through the rising waves. The stool began sliding as soon as she stood up, and Cado shut it into a cabinet. Isobel held onto the doorway, trying to keep her balance.

"I'd say we're in for a bit of rough weather," Cado said with relish. "I'll bet they'll be needing plenty of buckets for the passengers below. How's your stomach?"

"My stomach's fine," Isobel said, "but my legs are pretty wobbly. Do you think there's going to be a storm?"

Cado rested his large hands on the bottom door and stuck his head out the top half. He sniffed the air like a wary animal. "No," he concluded, "I'd guess it's just going to be a bit of a wagon ride. You'll be better off below, though, and I won't be needing you any more right now." He paused, stroking his beard and squinting at Isobel as if trying to make up his mind about something. "Hold on a minute. There is one more thing you could do for old Cado. Do you think you could bring some tea and biscuits to the captain and the helmsman?"

"I'm not sure," Isobel answered doubtfully. "To tell the truth, I could barely get here without grabbing onto everything that was tied down!"

"Well, you'll never get your sea legs if you don't force them out, and now's as good a time as any."

"Sea legs?" queried Isobel, lifting the hem of her skirt and looking dubiously at her thin legs.

"Even a girl as spindly as you has sea legs, if she'll only use them," Cado said. "Using your sea legs means getting used to walking about on the ship while the boat sways every which way under you. There are some sailors who can't find their land legs once the ship reaches port!"

"You mean they can't keep their balance on the ground? I can't believe it!"

"Well, it's as true as can be. Now, what do you say?"

"I'll try," Isobel agreed, but she remained skeptical.

Cado filled two heavy mugs with tea and covered the tops with inverted plates. He stacked them into a sack made of fish net. He dropped in four dry biscuits, and handed an extra one to Isobel. "You've got to get some pay," he laughed, and she devoured it in a few bites.

"Just walk straight back toward the quarter deck

after you bring the captain's tea," Cado directed her. "You'll find the helmsman sheltered in a little closet of his own. Hold onto the railing if you want, and you won't dance around so much. But if you just travel sure and steady your sea legs will carry you."

Isobel was pleased with her assignment to work in the cook room. She thought fleetingly of Padre Pão and wondered if all cooks were friendly. She stood up straight and tried to walk with confidence, but was glad that she had one free hand to help her climb the ladder to the captain's cabin.

The door was open when she reached it, but she knocked timidly on the door frame to get his attention. The captain motioned her toward his tiny desk and Isobel entered cautiously. The cabin was small and crowded. A bed hung from the wall by iron chains, and a short bookcase was packed with leather-bound volumes. There was a table piled with charts and a desk at which the captain sat, making entries in a blank book. A small round window with thick glass was set in the wall. Isobel could just make out the sails of another ship in the distance.

Isobel set the sack on the floor and carefully removed two biscuits, the saucer, and the tea. She tried to hold the cup steady as the ship rocked, afraid that she would spill the tea on the captain's papers. She sighed with relief as she successfully rested the cup beside the captain. He looked up, as if he were seeing her for the first time, and smiled at her, mumbling something in Dutch. Isobel smiled and backed out of the cabin.

Her job was going to work out. She had made the right decision not to depend on anyone but herself.

Now, if she could just find the helmsman. She was anxious to return to the families below. It is only that I am curious to see the preparations for the Jewish Sabbath, she told herself. It is not my celebration, but I would like to see it.

The area just below the quarter deck seemed deserted. Isobel looked about, worried that she might not have gone in the right direction. Then she saw a slatted door and heard someone coughing behind it. She stepped forward and knocked softly.

"*Sí!*" a man called, and Isobel stiffened. The man spoke Spanish! Yes, hadn't Cado told her that the helmsman and the first mate were Spaniards? Isobel entered cautiously. The room was nearly filled with a huge spoked wheel in front of which a burly sailor stood, gripping it tightly. There were two tall tables, both covered with maps and charts. A spyglass and a compass hung from a nail on the wall. She emptied the sack quickly and moved back out the door.

"*Grácias,*" grunted the helmsman in a raspy voice. "Thank you."

Isobel hurried back to find Maria Levy, forgetting that the empty sack dangled in her hand. Could the helmsman be one of the men she had overheard? There was no way for her to know, but she had to share her suspicions with Maria. She felt a cold chill as she made her way across the deck and she knew it had nothing to do with the gusting wind.

11

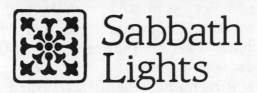 # Sabbath Lights

Isobel lifted her skirt slightly and climbed down the ladder into the passenger quarters. Babies cried, mothers scolded their children, and men talked in animated tones, but Isobel heard Rachelle's voice carrying above the din.

"You had no right to give it away!" She stamped her foot loudly. "You don't care at all about my feelings. You didn't even *ask* me!"

Maria answered her angry daughter with calm, reasoned words that Isobel could not make out. Still, she knew exactly what was bothering Rachelle. She looked down wistfully at the blue dress and traced the raised embroidery of the stomacher with her finger.

Rachelle stalked away with the air of a cat whose fur has been petted in the wrong direction. Isobel squatted down near the trunks, wishing there were some privacy. Clumsily she unhooked the dress fastenings and slipped the stomacher from its casing, trying not to look at the colorful embroidery. The polished cloth slid over her bare arms once again, and Isobel quickly pulled on her old frock with its familiar coarse brown fabric. She folded the white collar carefully and put it in her sack, but the apron seemed to soften the frock's shabbiness and left Isobel with at least a shred of similarity to the clothing worn by the other girls. She let her hair hang loosely over the hood and decided the lace cap would not be missed, even by someone as selfish as Rachelle. She moved to the spot where the girl had established her sleeping area, spread the dress out neatly, and walked away.

Davi was waiting for her when she returned, perched casually on the trunk lid with his long legs sprawled in front of him. He held a small pile of paper in one hand and a piece of black charcoal in the other. "And with a wave of her wand, the Fairy Princess transforms herself into a humble kitchen maid, so that only her true friends recognize her for the princess that she really is."

"Don't mock me, Davi," Isobel retorted. She stopped abruptly, surprised at her own outburst. But Davi was not put off.

"Your humble garments are a poor disguise. I can easily see that you are a real princess."

Perhaps Davi was not teasing her this time. She looked at him questioningly, her defenses gone. "Then you must be a true friend," she said quietly.

He began to sketch and Isobel watched in amazement as a tin lantern overhead reappeared in soft charcoal. Davi was now concentrating on his work.

The picture seemed to come to life under his graceful strokes.

"It seems our family is often apologizing for the rudeness of my sister," he said. "Believe me, she is not always this selfish, but perhaps she is a bit jealous."

"How could anyone be jealous of me?" Isobel asked.

"Maybe because of the attention you've gotten," he said, rubbing charcoal dust from his fingers. "Everyone is sympathetic to what you have gone through, and we all have spoken of your bravery in escaping. And perhaps Rachelle is afraid of the new place you have taken in our family."

"But I have no family here," Isobel protested. "I've tried not to depend on anyone. That's why I'm working for my passage."

Davi ignored her arguments. "You should keep the dress," he said.

"No. The dress doesn't matter," Isobel said, sitting down. She brushed some lint from her frock. "It would only have gotten soiled in the cook room, anyway. This old frock is used to hard work and doesn't seem to mind how dirty it becomes. Once I find my family I will throw it in the fire and happily watch it burn to ashes!"

Paulo caught sight of Isobel and wandered over, sitting close to her and rubbing his hand against her sleeve. "Yes, Paulo, I'm back in my old clothes again," she sighed.

"Another true believer, no doubt," Davi said with a wink.

Paulo looked with interest at Davi's sketch, then took other drawings from the pile and held them up for Isobel to see. A picture of Maria Levy's face made the biggest impression. Her eyes had the same kind look that Isobel had noticed, and her hair fell softly around her face. Her mouth had a sad, sweet smile. "How did you learn to draw like this?" Isobel asked.

"I haven't learned yet, really," Davi said. "When I get to Amsterdam, I am going to try to apprentice myself to a portrait painter. Good artists there are known the world over! But that is just a dream," he added. "My father says he needs me to work with him. Whoever heard of a butcher who was an artist?"

Paulo pointed to Maria setting up a makeshift table from a packing crate. Davi looked thoughtfully at Isobel. "I don't suppose you remember celebrating Shabbat, do you? Father says it is a time to put aside the cares and work that have occupied us during the week and allow our minds and bodies to rest. I really do feel different inside as soon as the Sabbath begins."

Isobel knew she would not feel any different. She would go on working in the cook room and wishing for the end of her journey. But she was curious about the celebration. Would the other passengers tolerate a Jewish ceremony right on the ship? She worried again about the men she had overheard talking about the Inquisition. She must tell Maria Levy. She had put it off too long.

But Maria was occupied with the preparations. A rough box was draped with a square of white linen whose four corners were embroidered with the blue six-pointed star that was a symbol of the Jewish religion. One day while they worked in the fields, her sister Maria had taught Isobel to scratch its shape into the soft earth. First Maria had drawn a triangle, and then she had etched an inverted triangle on top.

"This is the Star of David," Maria had explained solemnly. "I want you to remember it always." Then she rubbed out every trace before it could be discovered.

Emblazoned on the tablecloth, the symbol seemed strong and proud. Paulo's mother, Rachel Nuñes, placed a pair of polished brass candlesticks on the cloth, setting a white tallow candle in each. Sultana Lumbrusco placed a loaf of bread, twisted into a braided shape, between the candlesticks and covered it with a soft white linen napkin embroidered with unfamiliar lettering. Finally, a gleaming silver cup was filled with purple wine and set near the ceremonial items. The other passengers took little notice of the preparations, and Isobel thought they accepted them without concern.

"We usually have our best meal of the week on Friday nights," Davi said ruefully, "but with supplies so limited, we are lucky to have challah bread and soup. How many more weeks do you think it will be until there is a fresh roasted chicken, Paulo?"

For the first time, Isobel saw Paulo give a faint smile as he shrugged in answer to Davi's question. The thought of chicken made Isobel's mouth water. She was so hungry. She thought fleetingly of Padre Pão and imagined the smell of cooking that came from the church kitchen. No! she reminded herself. I'd rather be hungry than go back there!

"Come everyone," Asser Levy announced. "It is time to welcome the Sabbath Queen."

Members of the small Jewish community moved toward the table and gathered in a circle. Paulo held Isobel's hand, and Davi positioned himself near her, tucking his drawings carefully into his jacket. Traces of charcoal dust still clung to his fingertips.

Isobel tugged at Davi's arm and he bent lower. "Why does your father call the Sabbath a queen?" she whispered.

"It is an image that comes from a poem," he explained quietly. "It is because the Sabbath is beautiful and special, and because it is to be honored."

Isobel pictured a beautiful queen, like an angel, gliding down from Heaven and watching the ceremony.

Asser handed his wife a long glowing taper. Silence enveloped the group and the voices in the background were no longer an intrusion. Maria lit the two candles, extinguished the taper, and closed her eyes. Her hands hovered next to the candles, as if she were caressing their glow. She began to chant in a soft melodious voice and Isobel felt the prayer haunting her memory.

She closed her eyes, trying to remember. The image of another woman in another place floated across the distant reaches of her mind. Was she picturing her own mother, her head covered with a white lace mantilla, bending lovingly over the Friday night candles? She tightened her hand around Paulo's, feeling the warmth of his small fingers spread into the chill she felt in her own.

"All the blessings are in Hebrew," Davi said, "but they are simple. I could teach them to you sometime, if you'd like." Isobel was silent. Why would she learn Hebrew prayers? She did not know what to say.

Now Asser raised his hands in front of him, his long fingers close together and his palms slightly bent. The children all moved forward. Isobel held back, not wanting to intrude on the ceremony, but Paulo pulled her closer. She watched the children bow their heads and close their eyes. Asser chanted in Hebrew and then spoke in Portuguese: "The Lord bless you and keep you. The Lord make his face to shine upon you and be gracious to you. The Lord turn His face to you, and give you peace. Amen." The adults surrounding them added an uneven echo of amens. Isobel shifted uncomfortably from one foot to the other.

Abraham Israel raised the cup of wine and sang a blessing. He took a small sip and replaced the cup on the table. Judica Mereda handed her baby to Sultana, stepped to the place of honor, and gracefully pronounced the blessing for the bread. She broke off small bits of the loaf and passed them around as everyone turned to those around them with affectionate hugs and greetings of *"Shabbat shalom!"*

"I don't suppose you know what that means," Davi said. "It's Hebrew for 'Good Sabbath.' We wish each other a peaceful day of rest and a good week to come. *Shabbat shalom,* Isobel." Paulo tugged at Isobel's sleeve and nodded eagerly.

"Shabbat shalom, Paulo," she smiled, feeling the Hebrew words slide off her tongue as if it were a practiced habit.

The group began singing a lively tune as bowls of soup and pieces of bread were passed around. The glow of the candles reached every corner, and there was a feeling of peace that seemed almost tangible. But Isobel was absorbed in thought. Maybe, long ago, I had a family that welcomed the Sabbath like this, but all that is lost.

Paulo got up and returned, holding Isobel's burlap sack. He plunged his hand into it and pulled out the Bible.

"I had forgotten about that," she said. "My sister told me to read it when I felt lonely." Did Paulo know how lonely she felt right now? Even surrounded by all these people, I am still alone. If only Maria were here.

"You can read?" demanded a loud voice. Isobel was startled to see that Rachelle had joined them. "I never had time for such lessons. I'm surprised the friars allowed you to stop working long enough to learn."

"All of the children at the monastery were taught to read the Bible in Portuguese and also to read and recite the Latin prayers," she answered. "We had to learn."

"Paulo, come to bed," came his mother's voice. The child hesitated, looking at Isobel. Davi moved off to join the men, who were engaged in a lively discussion in one corner of the quarters.

"What's the matter, Paulo?" Isobel asked. The boy tapped the Bible and then pointed first to Isobel and then to himself.

"Do you want me to read to you?" she asked, and the child nodded. "If it's all right with your mother, I'll read after you are settled in bed."

"I'm going to listen, too." Rachelle announced.

Isobel did not answer. She picked her way among the sleeping mats spread out on the floor, and Rachelle boldly followed her. "Is it all right if I read to Paulo for a little while?" she asked Rachel Nuñes.

"As long as you don't keep him up too long, Isobel, I think it would be a great help. The sea is so rough tonight, it might keep his mind off it."

But Isobel did not think Paulo's mother would forget how the ship rose and fell heavily on the stormy waves. She seemed worried, as did many others. The passengers tied their trunks and bundles securely together to prevent them from being tossed about. Judica Mereda was steadying the candlesticks and debating with Maria whether it was safe to keep them burning, or if it would be a sacrilege to blow them out now. Isobel did not think she would be able to see the pages at all if the candles were extinguished. She had to begin while there was at least a little light.

"What shall I read?" she asked Paulo, and squatted down beside him, thumbing through the pages of the Bible.

"Anything," Rachelle cut in. "Just open the book and start."

Isobel ignored the girl's demand, but couldn't deny her own annoyance. "Do you like the story of Joseph and his brothers?" she asked the boy, pointedly turning away from Rachelle. He nodded sleepily.

Isobel strained her eyes in the dimness and read until she reached the portion where the brothers bring Benjamin, the youngest brother, to meet Joseph after he has become a powerful man in Egypt. None of them recognize Joseph as the brother they had sold into slavery. Isobel's voice was soft and clear and filled with emotion: "Joseph came close to Benjamin. 'God be with you,' he said gently. Benjamin looked up at Joseph and it struck Joseph how much like their mother the youth looked, and he felt near to tears because it had been a long time since he had been with his small brother. . . . And when the food was served, Benjamin was given five times that of his older brothers."

Isobel closed the Bible and looked down at Paulo. He was lying on his side, with his cheek resting on his hands. His eyes were half shut. She wondered if he were wishing that he could be reunited with his father, the way Joseph was reunited with Benjamin. She knew she would weep with joy if she could see her sister again. She smoothed the cover across Paulo's shoulders. "That's enough for tonight. Sleep well," she said. "We'll read the rest tomorrow."

Isobel picked her way toward her sleeping mat, with Rachelle trailing behind. As she walked around the trunk, she saw a mass of blue fabric laid out on her pallet.

"My mother says you're to have it," Rachelle said coldly. Isobel tried to think of the right words to say. She didn't want the dress if Rachelle had been forced to give it to her. There would be no joy in such a gift.

"I will save it for the day we arrive in Amsterdam," Isobel said. She folded it carefully and put it in the trunk.

Maria moved between the girls, smoothing covers and making sure there was no loose baggage. I should ask Maria about the sailors now, Isobel thought, but she still had doubts about what she had heard. If anyone on the ship was involved with the Inquisition, surely they wouldn't have let the Jews celebrate the Sabbath. Her memory of the conversation was less clear than before. Perhaps I was dreaming, she decided. Maria might think me foolish.

Maria knelt down and kissed her daughter good-night, and Isobel turned her eyes away, embarrassed to be watching. She thought of her own family and the time when they would be together again. *My sister and I will sleep in a big soft bed, piled with feather quilts,* she thought dreamily. *My father will read to us at night after we have dinner. A big dinner! Then my mother will kiss me goodnight, too.*

"Did you like the Shabbat celebration?" Maria asked, kneeling next to Isobel.

Isobel blinked into the growing darkness.

"That's not really a fair question, is it?" Maria said before Isobel could answer. "I know this is a painful time for you, Isobel. Your religion and your family must seem very far away. But time will change everything. Do not be impatient."

Isobel closed her eyes. *I wonder if Rachelle realizes how lucky she is to have her mother here. And Davi thought Rachelle was jealous of me!* She tried to concentrate on the time when she would find her own family and not feel envious of Rachelle when something unexpected happened. Maria bent over and kissed Isobel's cheek. "Good night, child. *Shabbat shalom.*"

 Changing Course

Isobel awoke with a start, blinking into the darkness that blanketed the passengers' quarters. She understood now that the cries and moans that disturbed her sleep were not part of a bad dream, but were real. Rachelle was moaning and doubled over. The ship pitched and rolled violently, and Isobel steadied herself against the trunk that bordered her sleeping mat.

"Rachelle, what's the matter?"

"It's my stomach," she answered hoarsely, as if every word were an effort. "I think I'm going to be sick."

Isobel remembered Cado's warning that the passengers were likely to become seasick during the storm. Her own stomach fluttered, but she felt she could control it if it did not get worse.

"I'll find your mother, and I'll get you a bucket," Isobel promised, although she did not know where she would find either one. She tried to stand, but her legs were more unsteady than her stomach. The ship seemed to hurl itself into every coming wave, and she thought that even sea legs would not help tonight.

She fumbled among the sleeping mats, trying to locate Maria. The hold was a mass of groaning, retching bodies bent over buckets and pails. A foul smell hung in the air, making Isobel's stomach roil about. She held her sleeve across her nose and mouth, trying to block out the sour odor. A few hardy souls seemed immune to the dip and toss of the ship, and they held buckets to the drooping heads of those less fortunate. Nothing around her looked familiar in the confusion, and Isobel wished she could run up on deck. But she had to find someone to take care of Rachelle first. With a sense of relief, Isobel happened on Davi carrying a stack of wooden pails.

"Rachelle is sick," she reported. "Where's your mother?"

"I'm afraid she's feeling the effects of the storm, too. My father is taking care of her. Can you bring this to my sister?" He separated one of the buckets from the pile.

"I guess so," Isobel answered reluctantly, taking the bucket from Davi. "Are you all right?"

"Steady as a rock, so far," Davi answered. "My mother always said I had a stomach made of stone. How about you?" He put his arm out to steady her as the ship gave a sudden lurch.

"My stomach isn't too bad, but I can barely walk."

"I knew you'd be all right. Who ever heard of a seasick princess?" He paused and then added, "Make sure Rachelle knows that this will pass. I mean, no one ever died of being seasick, did they? And, if you can, look in on Paulo."

"I'll try," Isobel said earnestly. Paulo clearly had developed a fondness for Isobel, and she felt a special tenderness for him. She still had not found out why he could not talk and determined to ask Davi as soon as she could. "Don't worry about Rachelle," she said, moving off. "I'll take care of her."

"Thank you," Davi called softly. "Thank you, *pequena irmã.*"

Did I hear him call me "little sister"? Isobel asked herself. She turned to look back at him, but he had disappeared into the darkness. It's been a long time since anyone called me that.

Isobel picked her way carefully back to where Rachelle lay, trying to hold her breath to keep from breathing in the awful smell.

"Don't try to talk," she said, squatting down beside Rachelle. "Here is a bucket if you need it. Davi says your mother is sick too, but your father is taking care of her. I know you're feeling awful, but it's just seasickness, and it will pass as soon as the storm does."

"I feel like I'm going to die," Rachelle moaned, but her complaint was interrupted by a fit of retching. Isobel couldn't help thinking that this was certainly the most distasteful job she had ever performed. She sat with Rachelle until the girl's stomach was empty and there was nothing for her to do but lie back and groan.

The shrill call of a whistle cut through the air, summoning the early morning crew on deck. Isobel was now part of the team that was expected to report for work, and she was grateful for the excuse to leave. She straightened Rachelle's blanket and added her own on top to keep off the damp chill that penetrated the quarters.

"I've got to go up and help in the galley," she explained. "Will you be all right for a while?"

"I'm so sick, I couldn't possibly get worse," Rachelle answered weakly, her eyes closed.

"Just rest," Isobel ordered. How had she ended up taking care of Rachelle? It hardly seemed fair. But, she told herself, she had done it for Maria Levy, who had cared for her so willingly. She turned to go, but Rachelle reached out a trembling hand and caught Isobel's sleeve. "Thank you," she said, almost inaudibly. "You didn't have to help me."

Isobel felt her anger and resistance against Rachelle flowing out of her like water from an uncorked bottle. She carefully moved across the quarters to where Paulo lay, and stooped down next to him. It seemed the worst had passed for him as well, but he was crying silently, big tears rolling down his cheeks.

"Everything seems pretty scary right now, Paulo, but the storm is already passing. And this is such a strong ship that a bit of rough weather can't hurt it. Why, it's just like floating a stick down a river. It bobs about when the waves hit it, but it never sinks." Paulo reached for her and Isobel held his small hand in her own. "You and your mother are feeling sick because people don't like being tossed around like sticks, but as soon as the storm is over, you'll both be fine again."

Paulo stopped crying. "I've got to work in the cook room," Isobel said, "but if you stay here and rest, I'll finish reading the story of Joseph and his brothers as soon as I'm done. How would that be?" Paulo nodded. "I'll be back before you know it."

She made her way up the ladder to the deck, hurrying to get away from the fetid stench that filled the passenger quarters, but she was unprepared for the weather that greeted her. A steady spray of drizzle dampened her face and clothes, and the wind whipped at her as she struggled across the wet deck. Isobel grabbed on to every rope, beam, and spar. Even an experienced sailor could lose his footing today, she thought. The door to the cook room was closed, and she banged on it several times before Cado opened the top half a crack.

"Oh, Izzy!" he laughed. "Well, I never expected to see you about in this weather. You must be a born sailor! Quick, come in where it's dry." He unlatched the bottom half of the door and she ducked in. "I see you came in work clothes today. What kind of a gown is this? Female clothes sure do puzzle me."

Isobel could not help laughing. "These aren't women's clothes," she teased the cook. "It's an old frock from the monastery. I don't have to worry about how messy this gets." She was relieved to be above deck, where a pot of mush was cooking and the spicy smell of brewed tea cheered her. "It looks as though you've got breakfast all cooked."

"The mush is mushed, all right," Cado joked, "but I've got to get some to the men who can't leave their posts. I'll need you to help me, but have some breakfast first."

Isobel looked at the huge pot of mush bubbling over

the fire and felt her stomach churn. "Maybe just some tea right now," she said, filling a tin mug.

"I can't believe you are turning down a good hot breakfast," Cado teased.

"Neither can I," Isobel remarked. "But being stuck down below didn't do much for my appetite." Cado ladled the lumpy mush into a wooden bowl and covered it with a plate. He set the bowl into another fish net sack and placed a small teapot carefully on top. Finally he dropped in an empty mug and a tin spoon.

"That should do it," he said as Isobel took the last few sips of her tea. "Take this to the helmsman. He's been at the wheel trying to keep this ship on course all night. I imagine there's nothing he'd be happier to see right now than his breakfast. Unless, of course, you brought along the sun and a fair wind!" Cado laughed his deep, self-mocking laugh and again flashed the shameless smile that revealed his missing teeth. Isobel took the bag, holding it firmly so that the tea would not spill, and opened the door. The rain had stopped, but dense fog surrounded the ship and rolled about the sails like playful ghosts.

She made her way toward the quarter deck, adjusting her pace to the ship's rolling. The tea had settled her stomach, and at least the wind smelled only of salt. Isobel hoped her sister's ship had fared well through the storm and that Maria had not become ill. She looked toward the ocean, trying to sight the companion ships, but all she could see was thick gray fog.

Isobel walked toward the slatted doors that led to the helmsman's cabin and she heard the sound of voices within. She hesitated before entering and realized the two men were speaking Spanish. She heard a cough and then a raspy voice. Isobel's heart seemed to stop beating for a moment. That was the voice she had overheard while hiding under the longboat! She had not imagined it.

"*Tienes éxito?*" came a demanding voice. "Have you succeeded?

"*Sí.*" The man with the raspy voice cleared his throat. "Yes. It's easy with this wind."

"No one knows?"

"No one."

The words that followed were rapid and whispered, and Isobel could catch only a few of them. Once again she heard the word *carabela*, something she still did not understand. The hateful sound of *La Inquisición*, and a new word, *los hebreos*, the Hebrews, were all too clear. Isobel tried to piece the fragments into a message that made sense. The helmsman was in charge of the maps and steering the ship. He had asked for ransom money and spoken of the Jews and the Inquisition. Would these men be planning something for so long, just to send her back to Recife? It didn't make sense. There had been so many opportunities for them to capture her. The captain wouldn't have stopped them.

No, she decided, it has to be something else. Something bigger and more important than me. As if someone had lifted a veil from Isobel's eyes, she suddenly thought she understood the plan clearly. The helmsman had agreed to steer the ship off course and arrange to turn all the Jews on board over to the Inquisition. The man giving orders must be the first mate. He must have arranged everything and expected a reward if it was successful.

If only I had told Maria Levy last night! she thought. She would have understood and perhaps we could have done something in time. What can I do now to stop this? Nearly everyone below is sick. I've waited too long!

The slatted door was pushed open by a thin, bony hand and Isobel found herself staring into the pinched face of a short man with a narrow moustache and sharp pointed beard. He was dressed in a black doublet and a long silken cape hung behind him and rustled at his sleeves. His eyebrows rose in surprise and anger when he saw Isobel. Isobel stepped back into a shadowy corner of the ship, afraid that the man would be alerted by her frock. This garment is a clear announcement that I am the child who escaped from the monastery, she thought. Then I surely will be turned over to the Inquisition.

"Qué quieres, niña?" he barked at her.

He was demanding to know what she wanted, but she pretended not to understand Spanish. She shrugged her shoulders and held up the net bag.

The man relaxed and motioned Isobel on as he hurried away. Isobel turned toward the doorway, but not before stealing a glance at the man's boots. They were of soft black leather with thin soles and a decoration Isobel had half-expected to see—shiny, filigreed silver buckles.

Isobel stepped into the helmsman's cabin and hurried to empty the sack and get away. She hoped that the navigator was too busy to pay her much attention.

Isobel set the food on one of the map tables and noticed that this morning all the instruments were strewn about on the table. A brass telescope lay across the charts, although Isobel could not imagine what anyone could see on such a foggy day. Silver instruments with curious writing and shiny dials rested nearby. As Isobel set the spoon down, she could not help noticing that a thick cross had been marked in red ink on the map. She could not understand its meaning, for she knew nothing of maps and charts.

She headed toward the door, but was caught at the entrance by the captain, who swept in angrily, wearing only his shirt and breeches. Without his doublet and plumed hat, he should have appeared less imposing, but his rage was more than enough to make up for his dress. He shouted loudly in Dutch, pounding on the maps and nearly toppling the teapot. He picked up a round instrument with a moving dial and shook it in the helmsman's face. The captain was furious.

The helmsman nervously cleared his throat and coughed twice, stammering out an answer to the captain's apparent accusations. Isobel pushed past the arguing men and bolted out the door. Something serious was happening, and there was no time to lose. She stopped on the deck, trying to decide what to do. The families below could not help her now. But perhaps she still had one friend who could. She raced to the cook room, ignoring the slippery deck and the tossing ship.

"Cado," she called breathlessly as she entered the galley, "what does *la carabela* mean in Spanish?"

"It's a kind of ship," he said, puzzled at her anxious

tone. "You can recognize one easily, for a caravel is rigged with triangular sails." He formed a shape with his hands, trying to make her understand. "The Dutch never use them. It's mostly the Spaniards and Portuguese who favor a caravel. Why, child? I certainly hope you didn't see one!"

Cado began stirring the mush again, but Isobel took the spoon from his hand and set it aside.

"Listen to me, Cado," she continued. "This is important. If someone wanted to change the direction of *The Valck*, do you think they could do it?"

"It wouldn't be easy," Cado replied. "The captain charts the course for the helmsman and if the course varied, he'd be sure to notice it right away. He'd be furious if the helmsman didn't follow the charts, probably put him below in irons! Besides that, we are traveling with fifteen other ships. We are always in sight of each other and any change in direction would be noticed by even the drunkest sailor."

Isobel thrust open the top of the double door and peered out into the lifting fog. Her eyes scanned the horizon for the companion ships.

"Cado," she said fearfully, her heart pounding in her chest. "They're gone."

The cook followed her to the doorway and looked out to sea. "No, child, it's probably just the fog hiding their sails. I'm sure they are out there." He put his hands on her shoulders. "You're trembling, Izzy. What's gotten into you?"

"Is it possible, just possible, that we could be off course and separated from the other vessels?"

"It may be that the storm blew us a bit off the

mark," Cado conceded, "but the helmsman is experienced with the charts and instruments. The fog is lifting rapidly, and the stars will be out tonight. He'll sight us back on course. Don't worry, child."

But Isobel would not let him go on. She put her hands on his muscular forearms, demanding all his attention.

"Listen to me, Cado. I think the helmsman and the man with the pointed beard have deliberately set us off course. I overheard them talking two times. I think they are planning to meet a Spanish caravel and turn the Jews over to the Inquisition."

The cook looked at Isobel gravely. There was no humor in his face now. "That's a serious charge," he said. "And a dangerous one."

"It could happen, though, couldn't it?" She gripped his arms more tightly.

"It's been known to happen, but we . . . "

"Be honest with me, Cado. What do they do?"

"There are Spanish and Portuguese privateers who will take Jews from traveling ships and sell them to the leaders of the Inquisition. They're like pirates, in a way, only they're dealing in people and ransom instead of treasure."

"Please tell the captain!" Isobel cried. "I've got to warn the others." She turned to unlatch the door, but Cado stopped her by holding it shut.

"Hold on," he cautioned. "You may be wrong, and if you are, you will cause needless panic. You are accusing the helmsman and the first mate of sabotage."

Isobel's mind was racing. Stop and think, a voice in her head repeated. But there was no time!

"Even if you are right," Cado continued, "you are not with the Jews, and no one will treat you as one. If you are asked, you must say you are Catholic."

"No! I could never do that."

"But you will be safe, and you'll get to Amsterdam."

Cado's words reminded Isobel of her reason for escaping. She had to find her family again. She remembered watching her sister walk down the road in Recife, refusing to say goodbye, and telling her that they would be together again in Amsterdam. Is that just a dream? she asked herself.

"Let me go, Cado," she said, pushing against the door. "I've got to warn the others!" The fog was dissipating, just as the cook had observed, and now that more of the ocean was visible, Isobel tried to see if any other ships were in view. As if by the power of her thoughts, she slowly made out the shape of another vessel looming up out of the misty air. Its bow was low in the water, its sails formed a triangular pattern, and its cannons were clearly pointed at *The Valck*.

Shouts rang out on the ship and sailors began running toward the cannon bays. "Spanish privateers," Cado muttered under his breath, as if not believing his own eyes. "By God, it's a Spanish caravel."

13

Attack of the Caravel

"Get inside!" Cado commanded. "Bolt the doors behind me, and don't open them until I tell you to." He slammed the double doors behind him and was gone.

Isobel slid the bolts into place and stared at the heavy oak door, studded with rusty bolts and cracked leather hinges. A loud report reverberated in her eardrums and shook the pots, the walls, and the very air around her.

Cannons! she thought in alarm. They're firing cannons at us! She fell to the floor and covered her head with her arms. "Oh, God," she breathed. "God of Isaac, God of Jacob, God of my fathers, help me." Isobel was bewildered by her own brief prayer. Her sister Maria had whispered it often, seeming to gain strength by remembering her faith's beginnings. The friars made me recite so many prayers, Isobel thought, but I only prayed with my mouth. Perhaps it was only her fear, but this time she felt a stirring in her heart.

There was a loud pounding on the door and Isobel jumped to her feet. "Izzy!" came Cado's urgent voice. "Open up!"

Isobel unbolted the doors and the cook rushed in, his head and shoulders bent forward and a bundle of clothes clutched in his hands. "There's breeches, shirt, vest, stockings, boots, and even a hat," he exulted. "You'll look exactly like a cabin boy. Take off your things and put these on. Quickly!"

Isobel's fingers fumbled at the apron tied about her waist until the knot was undone and the white linen fell to the floor in a soft heap. She pulled the frock over her head, knowing there was nowhere to hide in the tiny cook room even if she had demanded privacy. Cado gathered the brown shapeless garment into a ball and stuffed it into the fire, pushing at the reluctant folds with a long poker. Isobel watched with a mixture of joy and horror as the hated but familiar frock burst into flame. *I told Davi that I would happily watch it burn to ashes when I found my family. Where are they now?* Black smoke floated in the air as the flames licked at the coarse, dry fabric.

"Hurry!" Cado admonished her, and she pulled the stockings on and struggled into the short breeches, stuffing her long chemise into the loose-fitting pants.

"I think you'd better throw that underthing you're wearing into the fire, too," he added sheepishly. "You've got to pass for a boy now."

"No," Isobel said firmly. She pulled the shirt on as Cado bent down and laced a ribbon around the drooping stockings. "My sister made this for me, and I won't part with it." If Cado had argued, Isobel thought she might have to tell him about the precious combs, but he apparently did not want to discuss "underthings," and let the matter drop. She pulled a long brown vest over the cabin boy's shirt and buckled a stiff black leather belt around her waist. She slipped into a pair of tall boots, flexing her toes against the thick leather. Isobel took a few cautious steps and found she could move about in them more easily than in her sandals.

She thought fleetingly that she never seemed to wear clothes that were her own. First it was the friars' frocks that never fit, then Rachelle's borrowed gown, and now the breeches and boots of a cabin boy. My silver combs are the only things that are truly mine, she thought, and instead of wearing them, I must keep them hidden. She wondered what Davi would say if he saw her dressed as a boy. She doubted if he would call her a princess now.

The loud report of cannon fire thundered in the air, and Isobel noticed that the frightening sound of the battle had replaced the tossing of the ship. The seas were calm now, but the boat shuddered heavily each time a cannonball struck the water around it.

"I'm afraid your hair is too long, child," Cado said softly, as if afraid of upsetting her further. Isobel turned to the cook and saw that he gripped a long kitchen knife in his hand. "It is past your shoulders and it is sure to call attention to you."

"I can tuck it into the collar of my shirt," Isobel protested above the sound of shouts and cannon fire. "Or push it under the hat. Look," she offered, twisting her hair into one long hank and resting it on top of her head.

"No, Izzy, it won't do. It's got to be cut. Get down in front of the chopping block. I won't cut an inch more than I have to, and it will grow back in no time. Why, it's just like trimming your fingernails!"

Reluctantly Isobel knelt down and felt Cado pull her hair back in his large fist. Before she could change her mind, the dull thwack of the knife hit the wooden block. Cado looked defeated. His familiar smile was gone, and a forlorn, apologetic look replaced it.

"It's just hair, after all," Isobel managed to say, her voice quavering. She reached up and felt the blunt strands that prickled against her neck. Her head felt light, as if a weight had been lifted from it.

Cado deposited the fistful of silky black hair into the fire, where it singed and burned, leaving behind an acrid smell. The two of them stared after it.

"Things do not look good for us," Cado said, shaking his head. "The other ship took us by surprise. Our sails are already in shreds and the fight has only begun. The captain can't risk a direct hit to the hull. To be truthful, Isobel, *The Valck* can't hold out much longer, and you will be safest disguised as you are now. I think our attackers will let the crew and most of the passengers go. I must caution you about something, though." He put his hands on her shoulders and spoke slowly and earnestly. "You will not be able to talk to your friends and you must hope they will say nothing to you. It will go hardest with the Jews."

Somehow Isobel had always sensed the vulnerability of the small group of Jewish passengers. But she had not expected that she would be forced to shun them if she chose to remain with Cado.

"Maybe they'll leave the passengers," Isobel suggested. "Maybe they'll just take money and leave us alone!"

Cado shook his head emphatically. "Privateers aren't the same as pirates," he said. "For every Jew they turn over to the Inquisition, a handsome bounty is paid. If they also confiscate goods and valuables, the Queen will simply wink her eye. It's the Jews they want, don't you see?" What was most clear to Isobel now was that her failure to tell Asser and Maria about the plot she had overheard was responsible for the danger they were now in.

"I've got to get to them!" she shouted. "I've got to explain! It's all my fault. I should have warned them. I knew, and I didn't tell anyone."

"There's nothing they could have done, child. Even if you had told the captain, I doubt he would have believed you. He had charted our course along with the other ships. If he had noticed any change he would have blamed it on the storm. Even I didn't believe it was true."

Cado's words did not relieve the guilt Isobel felt. She thought of the times she had almost told Maria, but had been afraid to trust her. Then she remembered last night when she planned to tell her, but had not trusted her memory. She knew now that if she had confided in Maria, the captain would have been alerted. Perhaps he could have been convinced. The Jewish families had offered friendship and assistance and had asked nothing in return. She touched her cheek where Maria had kissed her goodnight. Because of her lack of faith, Isobel had betrayed them.

She looked at Cado with resignation. "Can't I even say goodbye?" she asked.

The cook opened his mouth to speak, but instead of his answer, Isobel heard the thundering boom of cannon fire and the sound of cracking timber. Cado lunged for her, pulling her down and nearly smothering her with his own lumbering body. The snap of splintering beams echoed in her ears and ended with a crash that rattled the ship from bow to stern. Pots and utensils tumbled off shelves and rolled about the floor, cabinets spilled their contents as if summoned by an invisible spirit, and a huge sack of dry beans split open as if it had been cut by a knife, sending beans bouncing across the floor like an army of invading ants. As the last pot stopped its clattering and the final bean rolled to a halt, an unnatural silence engulfed them. The ship sat still in the water. The storm had passed and the cannons were quiet. There was not even the sound of a wave splashing against the hull. Cado raised himself and lifted Isobel's head protectively, cradling her in his burly arms.

"Are you all right, child?"

Isobel grasped his arm and pulled herself to a sitting position. Her head was buzzing. "What happened?"

"I think they've struck the foremast, just in front of us," he said.

She looked around the tiny kitchen, littered with

utensils and spilled supplies. "How will we ever get this cleaned up?" she asked.

"We can't go anywhere without our mast," Cado said. "I think we have seen the last of this cook room, Izzy. And possibly the last of this ship."

 # Making a Choice

Cado unbolted the upper half of the double door and looked out cautiously.

"They won't fire at us again," he said with grim certainty. "They don't need to." He opened both portions of the door fully and stepped through.

Isobel followed closely behind. A few passengers peered nervously from the steps leading to their quarters. Without a word, members of the crew moved toward the foredeck. Isobel stifled a cry when she saw the reason. A young sailor lay crushed beneath the broken mast, his head turned sideways and his eyes staring blindly toward the stump of splinters.

She shivered at the horror of the scene. There was no blood; in fact, there were no marks of any kind on the young man. A look of surprise seemed to be on his face, as if he had not expected the mast to be hit.

A voice cut through the silence, barking orders in Dutch, and Isobel saw the captain stride across the deck. Two sailors scurried below, and several others lined up at the railing. A white flag was hoisted at the rear of the ship, next to the tattered remains of the ship's flag.

The captain leaned over the fallen sailor, closed the young man's eyes, and bowed his head in prayer. He pulled a white cloth from his doublet and placed it gently over the crewman's face. The arrogance Isobel had seen in the captain when she had first stolen onto the ship was gone, and she saw that he had added something to his blue doublet and cape. A long sword was fixed at his waist, encased in a heavy gold scabbard.

"See there?" Cado whispered in Isobel's ear, nodding his head toward the Spanish caravel. "They're coming aboard. Stay close to me and say nothing."

Fog and smoke still hung over the water between the two ships, but Isobel could make out three longboats cutting through the waves and approaching *The Valck*.

The passengers mounted to the deck, many still weak and unsteady from seasickness. As they crowded together, they assumed one identity. They look as frightened and confused as I am, Isobel thought. If I had been sick last night, I would be standing with them now.

She felt her stomach flutter as she searched for the familiar faces of Maria, Paulo, and Davi. She noticed Rachel Nuñes, but Paulo was not with her. She spotted him standing forlornly near a Dutch colonist. Sultana Lumbrusco was near the railing, but Mose was not nearby. Instead of standing as a group, the Jews had split their families and mixed in singly with their fellow passengers. They are trying to keep from being noticed, she realized. They are hiding, as I am.

"Arriva! Arriva!" shouted the Spanish sailors as their longboats hit the side of the ship with heavy thuds. As the Spaniards clambered up rope ladders over the railing, the Dutch sailors stiffened, but held their posts.

A slight movement caught Isobel's eye, and she noticed that the first mate, holding his long cape close to his sides, was moving furtively along the outside railing. A slight, almost imperceptible smile played across his lips and gave him a look of haughty disdain. The image of another small and disdainful man entered her thoughts. Take away the first mate's pointed beard, his fine clothes and filigreed boots, and dress him in a humble frock and sandals, she thought, and he has the same self-satisfied look as Padre Francisco. They would be in total agreement with the plan to turn the Jews over to the Inquisition.

The Spanish privateers boarded the ship. Their faces were dark and angry, and they drew their swords and waved them in the air menacingly. Isobel shrank closer to Cado and watched fearfully as the captain of the conquering caravel, wearing garish green breeches and a red and green brocade doublet, strode confidently to the captain of *The Valck*. The Dutch captain looked unflinchingly at his victor and unbuckled the sword and scabbard that hung at his waist. Without giving away his pride, Isobel saw him hold the sheathed weapon in his outstretched hands. With a nod of mock humility, the Spanish captain lifted the sword with one hand and laughingly tossed it to one of his men.

A breeze blew away the last wisps of fog, and the sun sent its rays through the ragged sails.

"I extend my sincere gratitude," the captain began, speaking loudly in Spanish and enunciating each word. He must think he's speaking to someone who is deaf, Isobel thought. The captain may not understand Spanish, but it certainly isn't necessary to shout. The first mate appeared at the privateer's side and began translating into Dutch, occasionally pausing to whisper in the Spaniard's ear.

"Señor Vasquez, your able assistant, has been most helpful in bringing us together," continued the gaudily dressed captain, and his men erupted in loud and raucous laughter. "May I assure you that neither you nor your crew are in any further danger. In fact, we would like to help your ship along its way by lightening its load. My men will pass among you and accept donations of jewelry and coin. It would be most difficult to proceed with heavy cargo without the advantage of a foremast." The Spaniard smiled broadly, and his teeth flashed white against his tanned and weathered face. Once again, his sailors roared approval of the captain's sarcastic humor.

The privateers began moving among the passengers and crew, rudely pulling gold necklaces, earrings, and rings from them. An elderly colonist was roughly stripped of his coat and pushed to the deck. With one swift stroke, a privateer slashed his blade through the velvety cloth, shouting in triumph as a shower of gold coins spilled from the lining and bounced onto the deck. Isobel prayed silently that she would not be searched. How did the Spanish sailor know the man had sewed coins into his coat? Other Spanish crewmen went below deck to search through trunks and baggage for items of value.

The commander of the caravel put his arm around the first mate's shoulder in an intimate and trusting gesture.

"Señor Vasquez tells me you are also overloaded with passengers." He paused. The moment seemed interminable. Isobel felt her pulse quicken, and she held her breath waiting for him to continue. "Some excess baggage, we might say, involving heathen Jews." The privateer lingered over the last word, drawing it out to emphasize his distaste. He turned his head and spat loudly on the deck.

The first mate withdrew a rolled parchment from under his cape and handed it to his compatriot. The captain unrolled it slowly. "Six heads of families and various assorted wives and children, I believe." His look was hard, but the smile still flashed across his face. "And where might these damned souls be found?"

The captain made no answer and fixed an accusing stare at the first mate. A Spanish crewman marched across the deck holding a heavy scroll wrapped in deep burgundy velvet and embroidered in thick gold threads. Engraved silver ornaments like tiny crowns topped the wooden dowels at its two ends. With such rich decoration, it had to be something of great value. A second privateer ducked into the cook room and emerged holding a stick whose end had been ignited in the stove. He lifted his makeshift torch toward the scroll. There were gasps among the passengers.

"You see how easy it is to find these Jews," the victorious captain explained. "They will risk their very lives to protect this written evidence of their heathen religion."

It's a Torah, Isobel realized as her memory flashed to an image of men crowded around a high table, lifting a scroll high in the air. Someone had picked her up so she could see it. The Torah had been part of her life before she had been taken away. She remembered it!

The captain's voice rose to a shout. "Let all the Jews step forward to their scroll of lies, or let them watch it burn to ashes!" The crewman obediently moved his torch a few inches closer to the velvet covering. Isobel froze. They were going to burn it! A singed spot appeared on the edges as the heat intensified.

"No!" came an anguished cry, and Asser Levy pushed his way through the passengers.

The Spanish captain let out a derisive laugh. "Heathens and fools!" he declared. "Let the Jews come forward for their satanic writings and let the courts of the Inquisition judge them!"

Singly and in pairs, some clutching each other in fear, the families who had welcomed Isobel a few days earlier came toward the captain of the caravel. Paulo ran to his mother and clung to her arm. His face was pale and his thin shoulders visibly trembled. Maria followed anxiously after her husband, but walked proudly with her back straight and her head high. As Davi walked forward, his glance fell on Isobel. A puzzled expression crossed his face and then his eyes widened. In a fleeting second, so fast that Isobel barely saw the change, a look of sadness filled his eyes and he turned his head away.

Isobel wanted to cry out. Wait, she wanted to say, this wasn't my idea! She thought she would gain her freedom by escaping from the friars, yet she was still following orders. But I have no choice, she reasoned. I am only twelve.

The words sounded in her head, but the voice was not hers. It was her sister Maria's, repeating words she had told Isobel in the quiet barn in Recife. "I was a child when I stepped onto that boat, and I became a woman as soon as it sailed, for there was no more time to be a little girl." For the first time, Isobel was faced with a true choice. She was not a child any longer. And she could be free. But if she truly wanted to take responsibility for her own life, she had to follow not just her head, but also her heart.

She saw Vasquez whispering to his commander with a pleased look on his face. "There seems to be a small matter of a stowaway," the Spanish captain said questioningly. The captain of *The Valck* remained silent. "A young child, I'm told, who has been cared for by the Jews." There was a weighty pause, and then he continued. "Is this child a baptized Christian or a Jew?"

A heavy silence hung in the air. Then Isobel heard the sound of her own voice as she took a step forward.

"A Jew," she said firmly. This time, she was in control. She sensed that Cado was about to pull her back and she stepped quickly away from his reach, trying to save him any punishment for trying to hide her.

The Spanish captain swung around and glared at her as she walked toward him. "A boy?" he asked with surprise. He turned to the first mate. "I thought you said it was a girl child?"

Isobel did not give Vasquez a chance to answer for her. "Not a boy and not a child. I am Isobel Ben Lazar, daughter of Abraham Ben Lazar, once advisor to the king of Portugal. I am a Jew and I am a woman."

The captain let out a bellowing laugh. "A woman? A woman with cropped hair and breeches?" His men and the first mate joined in his joke, but Isobel did not flinch. Let them mock her. Even if they held her captive, she was freer than she had been in six years.

She moved into the group of Jewish families. She was a part of their circle, part of them. A hand squeezed her shoulder. She turned and saw that it was Davi. A look of respect filled his eyes. He inclined his head toward her ear and whispered, "In any disguise, still a princess."

 New Prisons

A pattern of square grids from the hold above shadowed the faces of the Jews as if a thick net had been thrown over them. They huddled beneath the opening, for it provided the only source of light and air in the dank area beneath the deck of the caravel. The strong smell of rum and beer rose from the floor boards and mingled with the odor of sweating bodies.

The thought of *The Valck* haunted Isobel. Could the ship sail without its mast? Was Cado worried about her?

Isobel looked at the pale, listless faces of her friends. Several dozed uncomfortably, their heads propped on their neighbor's shoulders or laps. The shouts and scuffles of the privateers on deck frightened her into a restless vigil. She felt the warm closeness of Paulo curled up alongside her. No matter what might befall her now, she would not have to face it alone.

In the dreary sameness of the days, Isobel lost all

sense of time. Daylight and darkness blurred together.
The privateers fed them irregularly and gave them only
enough food to keep them alive. Hunger gnawed at her
stomach as she thought of the dry biscuits and stale
beer that were lowered to the Jews in a bucket. The
children had gagged at the first taste of the provisions,
but Asser offered prayers thanking God for bread and
for wine. Although his words did not change the sour
taste, it had made them remember to be grateful for
any sustenance.

Baruch atoh adonai . . . blessed art thou, oh Lord.
. . . The words came back to her and soothed her even
as she chewed the hard, tasteless bread. Is it possible,
she thought, that I am learning to be a Jew even in this
horrible place?

There had been little talking since the capture, only
a fearful, quiet waiting. What would the others say if
they knew that I could have saved us, Isobel wondered.
If only I had trusted them—and myself. How can I ever
tell them? She held her secret uncomfortably and it
pricked at her conscience as the silver combs pinched
at her sides. She reached up and felt the uneven ends
of her cropped hair. I shouldn't have let Cado try to
disguise me! Now it will be months, maybe years,
before I can wear my combs. Then Isobel remembered
what the privateers intended to do with her and the
others. I will certainly have no use for silver combs if
the Inquisition sends me back to the monastery.

There was a creaking sound at the grate overhead
and Isobel looked up. Two unshaven privateers pulled
it open and dropped down a ladder. A shaft of sunlight
streamed in.

"*Arriva!*" shouted one of the pirates. He cracked a whip just above their heads and they scattered in terror. He bent his face over the hold and called out with a leering smile, "*Bienvenidos a Cuba!*"

Asser looked startled. "We're in Cuba!" Isobel's ears picked up the word she had not understood when she had overheard the helmsman and the first mate.

"What are they going to do with us?" Rachelle demanded plaintively. "Where are we?"

Asser began gathering their few remaining possessions. "It's a small island," he said. "I don't know why they've taken us here."

"I don't think the Spaniards have a colony here," Judica said. "Maybe the privateers have come for fresh water and provisions. Asser, help me wrap the Torah in the bedding. If they are taking us ashore we must try to keep it as dry as possible." As they folded blankets around the scroll, Isobel noticed the singed, black spot that remained on its velvet covering.

Paulo followed close behind as Isobel made her way up the narrow ladder. She still wore the breeches and vest that Cado had given her, and she realized that she now looked like the child's brother, not his sister.

The smell of salt water and green trees permeated the warm air. "It's strange," she confided quietly to Paulo, "but I think I'm looking forward to standing on firm ground again, even if it is Cuba and not Holland." The boy brightened a bit.

The privateers ferried the prisoners ashore in three longboats and landed in a hidden harbor with a broad sandy beach bordered by trees and shrubs that resembled those in Recife. Isobel detected the sweet odor of sugar cane blowing on the breeze. The helmsman and first mate were already on shore, and they supervised the prisoners, looking smug.

"*Arriva!*" wheezed the helmsman in his raspy voice, motioning the group toward a narrow, brush-covered path. They dragged their trunks and baggage while the sailors urged them on.

"My legs feel wobbly," Rachelle complained. "I need to stop and rest."

"*Silencio!*" commanded one of the sailors, giving Rachelle a rough push. She glared angrily at him as if she expected an apology, but he merely turned his back indifferently. Shortly they came to a small compound surrounded by a high stockade. Their captors herded them inside and swung the heavy gate shut. Isobel and the others stood still listening to the sound of a crossbar being fitted into place, followed by the raucous sound of satisfied laughter. Isobel shuddered to think that the first mate's plan had been so successful.

Inside the fenced area, the ground was well trampled, and only a few patches of grass sprouted in isolated corners. Twigs and branches from overhanging trees littered the dirt. There were four small huts with thatched roofs and a well for water. There was no one else in sight—no privateers, no natives, no colonists.

As the exhausted group stood in silence, Isobel felt a cold trembling creep down her back and along her arms. This is what I have chosen, she reminded herself. It is what I had to do. I can't give up or I am truly lost. She turned her attention to the stone well that stood in the center of the compound. A bucket hung from a rope and dangled invitingly over the water.

"I don't know about anyone else," Isobel said, startling even herself with the sound of her voice, "but I'm going to fill that bucket and drink until I can't drink any more." She dropped the bundles she had been carrying and proceeded toward the well. "Come on, Paulo," she called over her shoulder. "It's fresh water! Aren't you thirsty?"

"I want a bath!" shouted little Estrella Lumbrusco. Her emerald-green eyes sparkled with anticipation as she pulled at her mother's skirt. "Mama, find some soap!"

"Oh," sighed Rachelle. "I could wash my hair. Sultana, I must borrow your soap."

"We ought to wash ourselves and our clothes while there's fresh water," Davi said. "We could be moved from here at any time." He sniffed at his sleeve and made a disgusted face. "Ugh! I smell like stale beer. God knows, we could all use a bath!"

"God must know," said Abraham's son Franco, "for surely the smell reaches all the way to Heaven!"

The pall of resignation that had gripped them broke. Davi, Franco, and the older boys were dispatched to collect dry sticks for a fire, and the adults set off to check the huts for any useful items.

At first the children took a few polite swallows of the cool water, but soon they began to dunk their hands into the bucket, rubbing their dusty faces and necks. It wasn't long before they began flicking droplets at each other. Soon the boys were chasing after the girls with water dripping from their cupped hands. The girls let out squeals of delight, racing around the huts so they would not be splashed.

Davi came up to the well carrying an armload of small sticks. "We were shut in that smelly hold for so long, I thought we had surely forgotten how to run at all." He leaned against the well and his face grew serious. "I know I haven't suffered as many changes as you, but it seems years since I left Recife, instead of weeks. I feel as if so many pieces of my life have just disappeared. It's as if all my drawings had just been erased."

"At least you still have your family," Isobel comforted him.

Davi shifted the wood in his arms uncomfortably. "You are part of our family, too, you know." He paused and then said, "I did not expect you to come with us. You didn't have to make that choice." He pounded his fist on the stone well. "If only we could escape and get to Amsterdam, I think we could help you start a new life."

"I thought you hated me for trying to hide," she stammered.

"I would never blame you for trying to survive, and I knew the disguise could not have been your plan."

Isobel looked down at her boots. She felt embarrassed and confused. "I feel so stupid in these clothes. And my hair . . . "

At this Davi laughed. "My father says change is what makes us grow. Your short hair is a symbol of your change. Now you are choosing your own life, your own people."

"Davi! Hurry with that wood!" called Asser. A small

fire had been started, and he approached with a pot to fill at the well.

"I must go, little sister," Davi said. "Who knows, perhaps the change in your hair will make it grow, too!"

Asser lowered the bucket into the well. He pointed to one of the shelters close to the fence. "Our family will share that hut with Paulo and Rachel Nuñes. Rachel asked if they could stay with us, since Paulo has become so fond of you. Go and bathe now, while it is still sunny enough to dry your hair."

"Asser," Isobel interrupted, "what is wrong with Paulo? Why can't he talk?"

"I'm not sure, child, but I think it was the shock of his father's death." He pulled up the full bucket and tensed slightly. He spoke briskly of Paulo's father and tried to conceal his emotions, but Isobel sensed the pain he felt.

"Aharon Nuñes was at the synagogue when the Portuguese soldiers took it over for their barracks. We think he may have tried to fight them off, although he was alone and had no weapons. When we found his beaten body, we could barely recognize him."

"But what about Paulo?" Isobel asked.

"Paulo was missing after we discovered Aharon. We searched everywhere for him, without success. The next day he suddenly appeared at his mother's door, dazed. He didn't cry or say where he had been. He simply never said another word."

"How did he know about his father?" Isobel asked.

"He must have been at the synagogue when his father was killed. We don't know how much he saw.

Perhaps he felt that he should have helped his father, but of course, he couldn't have done anything." Isobel turned and walked toward the hut, wondering how she could help Paulo.

After the children had washed, they put on whatever clean clothes could be found. The privateers had taken every item that had any value, but they'd left some clothes, bedding, and a few personal belongings that did not interest them. All the religious books were left untouched, and although the group was thankful, they feared that the reason was not respect but a chance to provide evidence to the Inquisition that the captives were infidels.

Several trunks had been lost in the transfer between ships, and Rachelle's clothes were among the items missing. The two girls sat on a blanket, drying their hair in the sun. Rachelle looked with dissatisfaction at the simple homespun cloth of the borrowed dress she now wore. "I can't believe I have no clean collars and none of my embroidered chemises," she complained. "It's not fair!"

Isobel ignored her whining. Since the night she had helped Rachelle through her seasickness an unspoken truce had existed between them. She smoothed the folds of the dress she wore and lifted her face toward the sun as it dropped lower in the afternoon sky. "With this dress to wear instead of breeches, I feel so much better. Even my hair doesn't seem so bad now that it's clean. It may not sound sensible, but I don't feel like a prisoner at all."

"All the rest of us do!" Rachelle insisted. "Just look around you. Surrounded by a stockade, guarded by pirates, and on our way to be judged by the Inquisition!"

"I don't know why, Rachelle, but I can't give up hope that we are going to make it safely to Amsterdam. Maybe it's because we're off the ship and left on our own. It's just a feeling. . . . "

"I wish there was some reason to believe you," Rachelle began, when Paulo ran up to them with a book in his outstretched hand.

"Paulo," Isobel exclaimed. "Where did you find my Bible?" Paulo handed her the book and sat down expectantly at Isobel's feet.

"I think he's waiting for you to finish the story about Joseph and his brothers," Rachelle said. She turned to Isobel. "I want you to teach me to read. Papa thinks we're going to be here for at least a week while the privateers stock their ship. It would give us something to do!"

"It takes more than a week to learn to read!" Isobel answered. Rachelle could be so annoying. Then she thought for a moment. Perhaps if she had something to share with the girl they could learn to get along better. Now that she had joined the Jewish families it was more important to settle her differences with Rachelle. "I'll start teaching you to read," she offered, "if you'll teach me how to embroider." Paulo pulled at Isobel's sleeve and gestured emphatically to himself. "You too, Paulo," she laughed. But then she added silently to herself, if only you'll start to talk.

"All my sewing things were in my trunks," Rachelle pouted. "But I'll teach you to embroider as soon as I can. I promise!"

Isobel smiled at the girl. "It's settled, then," she announced. She thumbed through the Bible, searching for the story that had been left unfinished.

"We were at the part where Joseph gives Benjamin more food than his other brothers," Rachelle recollected. "Why does he do that? There was a famine in Egypt and since Benjamin is the youngest, he probably can't eat nearly as much as his older brothers, anyway."

"It has nothing to do with his appetite, I can tell you that," interjected an impatient voice. "It was a sign of honor."

"Oh, Davi, who asked you?" Rachelle scolded her brother. "You think you know everything!"

Davi sat down near Paulo and pulled out his paper and charcoal. "Well, I have studied Torah. This story has been discussed many times."

"Who cares about your Torah classes?" Rachelle retorted.

"Never mind, then," Davi conceded. "Finish the story, Isobel." He began to sketch while Isobel read.

She continued where she had left off. The story flowed in her clear, emotion-filled voice. She read about the trap that Joseph laid, how the brothers were brought back and charged with stealing before Joseph revealed himself. Finally, Joseph was reunited with his father. Isobel saw tears forming in Paulo's eyes as she read the story to its conclusion. "And Joseph presented himself unto him, and they wept a good while. And his father said unto Joseph: 'Now let me die, since I have seen thy face, that thou art yet alive.'"

Isobel closed the book and no one spoke. Tears

streamed down Paulo's cheeks and his shoulders shook with sobs, yet not a single sound came from him. Isobel drew the boy into her arms. "You have lost your father, but still you have your mother. Think how much she loves you. Each of us has lost something, but we are together here and perhaps that is enough."

Davi spoke. "Joseph's father felt he could die in peace knowing that his son was alive and safe. I believe your father would feel the same, Paulo."

The child burrowed his head deeper into Isobel's arms and closed his eyes tightly. She did not know if he understood Davi's words, but she knew he had heard.

Davi put down his drawing. "It is good for him to cry, I think. It's the first time he has let his feelings show since his father . . . " His voice trailed off.

Isobel cradled Paulo in her arms until the sobs faded. He seemed so small, so fragile. She felt she had grown since she left the monastery, both in size and in age. Am I still only twelve? she wondered.

There was some commotion near the gate, and Isobel turned her head to look. "Maybe the privateers are bringing us food," she told Paulo. "Can you tell?"

Paulo raised his head and wiped at his swollen eyes. Isobel sensed the tiredness that had come after his tears.

A group of five natives, dressed in brightly colored clothes, entered the compound. They were accompanied by six sailors from the caravel, who acted as guards. The dark-skinned natives resembled the Brazilians who had brought food to sell at the monastery in Bahia. The women wore long printed dresses and covered their black hair with patterned scarves. They all carried baskets of fruit and foods that made Isobel's mouth water.

"Look, Paulo! Bananas and pineapples and oranges! I was afraid they wouldn't bring us any food at all. I think I've forgotten what fresh fruit tastes like!"

A man stepped forward carrying a large basket filled with rice, and a small bowl. He scooped up a bowlful of grain and held it up.

"*Riz,*" he said, his bearded face crinkling into a mass of smiling wrinkles. "What you pay? Is good. No bugs!" He let the rice in the bowl pour down in a tempting cascade.

Rachel Nuñes stood by Paulo and Isobel, her arms folded across her chest and her face set in a grim look. "They capture us, they steal nearly everything we have, and then they expect us to pay for our keep! What do they think we have left for payment?"

Isobel thought guiltily of the silver combs hidden in the seams of her chemise. She did not want to give them up. She shifted uncomfortably on her seat.

Gloria, the chubby, smiling wife of Abraham Israel, did not seem as concerned as Rachel. "We may yet have something to offer these natives," she said. She walked briskly toward the traders as her sons, Avram and Franco, carried a small trunk between them. At a signal from their father, the boys opened the heavy lid, revealing a glittering heap of brass berimbaos. The natives were puzzled, but obviously intrigued with the shiny objects. The boys put the simple instruments to their mouths and played a lively tune.

The natives laughed and clapped their hands in time

to the mellow, vibrating notes that filled the air. Abraham demonstrated how the berimbao was used. Then he held up a new instrument from the trunk. *"Uno berimbao,"* he said, gesturing to the food, *"uno porción de riz."*

Then the bartering and trading began. Baskets of food and berimbaos changed hands, and in a short time, the natives left and the group gathered up the provisions just purchased. Once again the gates were shut and a heavy bar dropped into place.

"Thank you for caring for Paulo, Isobel," said Rachel kindly as she led him toward the hut. "God sent you to us. I know he did."

Isobel put the Bible into her pocket and went to help with the evening meal. Dinner passed with prayers of thanks for the group's continued safety and for the food they had received.

"I am exhausted," Sultana complained, "and the children are nearly asleep on the ground." She got up slowly and brushed the dirt from her dress. Mose yawned.

Isobel followed the other children toward the huts but noticed the adults stayed near the fire, talking quietly.

"Why aren't they going to bed, too?" Rachelle asked.

"They are trying to find a way to escape," Davi said softly. "We can't let the privateers take us to Spain."

"I think we are safe here, Davi, don't you?" Isobel asked.

Davi hesitated before answering. "Maybe," he said. "But someone will stand watch at each hut. Don't forget that the gate opens only from the outside."

Isobel hugged her blanket close as the air cooled. There were no rocking waves, no creaking boards, only the sound of frogs croaking to each other in the darkness and the silence of her thoughts. *Paulo may feel responsible for not saving his father, but I am the one who let everyone here be captured. I have to find a way to make up for it.*

She remembered her dream of finding her sister and her family in Amsterdam. *I have not forgotten you, Maria. I pray you are safe and that God has watched over you.* Isobel's eyes closed and she felt as if she were floating above the hard earth and above all the difficulties and danger of the days that had come before, and the days that would surely follow. *I will find you, Maria. I will.*

Temporary Shelter

Isobel sat in the shade, looking at the children seated about her. She scratched a letter into the dirt with a stout twig and a chorus of voices called out "P!" Two weeks ago they had barely known their letters, and now they were beginning to read. She erased the letter with the side of her hand and drew again. "S!" came the voices.

"I got it first! I know I did!" shouted Luis Lumbrusco. He squirmed around, waving his arms in the air and kicking his feet against the ground.

When Isobel began teaching Rachelle and Paulo to recognize the letters of the alphabet, a few other children joined them. There was Luis and his sister Estrella, who was only six but who learned as quickly as the others. Ten-year-old Marcella Israel concentrated seriously on every word Isobel said, her thick hair falling across her tiny face. Her younger sister Gracia was eight and learned more slowly, but still she learned. Her pudgy face seemed always to be breaking out into a grin and then a giggle.

"Today we're going to go over some of the words we learned yesterday," Isobel said, opening her Bible. "Here, Rachelle. You start."

"Oh, Isobel, I can't read it unless you help me."

"I'll help if you need me," Isobel said. "Just read a couple of words."

Rachelle took the small Bible and began to read. Her voice was soft and hesitant, so unlike her usual demanding tone. Rachelle's attitude seemed to improve when Isobel brought the children together. She seemed willing to be part of the group instead of always in charge of it.

"That was good," Isobel said. "Now, let's hear from Estrella." Rachelle passed the Bible to the younger girl. Estrella's energetic voice grasped the words and sounded them out with careful clarity.

"And . . . God . . . said . . . " Then she giggled.

"What about you, Paulo? Are you ready to try?" Paulo lowered his eyes and shook his head. I know he understands the lessons, and I've seen him following the words with his eyes. "That's all right," she said calmly. "You be the pointer finger, and I'll be your voice." Paulo looked at Isobel gratefully. So far, the boy still had not spoken. Yet she was not totally discouraged.

Each of the children read in turn, practicing the words over and over until their reading became smoother.

"Pretty soon the only child in this camp who won't

know how to read will be baby Rayna!" she said. They all laughed and patted each other on the back.

Avram and Franco came up to them, with Davi right behind. "Are you ready for your music lesson yet?" Avram asked. The children stood and stretched and then brought out the berimbaos that the de Piza family had given them. Isobel had not only started the reading lessons, but also persuaded the de Piza boys to teach them to play the brass musical instruments their father crafted.

It did not take long for the children to learn to control the breathing and plucking that combined to make a melody reverberate through the air. Today, the melow, twanging notes blended into one vibrating tune. Isobel treasured her berimbao and thought the music helped everyone feel calmer and more cheerful.

"Let's play for everyone tonight," Estrella piped up.

"Why not?" Rachelle joked. "Our parents are pretty hardy. I think they can survive our music!"

With the lessons over, the children ran off, but Paulo wandered away slowly, his eyes fastened on the Bible. His finger pointed to the printed words and his lips moved silently.

Davi walked with Isobel toward the area where the evening meal was being prepared. "Has Paulo broken his silence yet?" he asked.

"No," Isobel sighed. "I keep feeling he will, but nothing changes."

"Perhaps if we had made it to Amsterdam, he might have been able to put his fears behind him."

"This may not be the safety of Amsterdam," Isobel

responded, "but we are better off than we were on the Spanish ship."

"Isobel," Davi said, "I'm afraid the life you seem to think is so peaceful here is just an illusion. You are probably wasting your time with reading lessons. In a few days the ship will be stocked with provisions and we will be herded like goats back into the hold."

Isobel turned her face away from Davi to hide the fear his words brought.

"I must believe that somehow things will work out. There has to be a reason for us to keep going."

"I don't know why I bother to draw anything. It's useless," Davi argued. "Everything we do is useless."

Isobel felt Davi's sense of defeat. "Why can't we all try to escape? There must be a way."

"Father and the others have discussed every possible idea," he said, "and they don't believe it can be done. They've been planning since we arrived. But what can we do? There aren't enough of us to overpower a whole crew of armed privateers and, even if we escaped from this compound, what good would it do to run into the jungle?"

"It's all my fault," Isobel blurted out. She covered her face with her hands and shook her head. "I heard the plan and I didn't tell anyone!"

Davi grasped Isobel's arm. "What are you saying?"

"When I was hiding under the longboat, I heard two men talking in Spanish. I couldn't understand exactly what they were saying, but I knew they were talking about the Inquisition and about something happening in a week. I thought they were talking about capturing me and sending me back to the monastery. By the time I realized what was happening, the privateers had already attacked us."

Davi dropped his hold on Isobel's arm. Several long moments passed before he spoke.

"You couldn't have known, Isobel," he said finally. "Don't blame yourself any more." Davi ran his hands impatiently through his hair. "You trusted us by coming forward on the ship. We're the ones who have failed you. In a few days we will sail directly to Madrid. That's the only reason the privateers have given us food. We are worth payment by the Inquisition only if we are alive enough to be burned!" He shook his head. "You should have stayed on *The Valck*."

"Even if you're right, Davi, it doesn't change things for me. I've got to make up for what I've done! It only makes the reading lessons and the music more important. Don't you see?"

Isobel did not wait for an answer, but hurried over to Maria. "Can I help?" Isobel asked.

"I can always use help," Maria smiled, and handed her a yellow and green pineapple. Isobel began cutting the thick rind.

Without looking up she said, "Davi thinks I am foolish for teaching the children to read. He's convinced we will all be dead before long."

If Maria was shocked by Isobel's blunt words, the only hint was a momentary hesitation. "We will all die some day. That is part of life. Does that mean we should give up before that moment comes? I don't think Davi means that. Every time I see him he is bent over a drawing. But we have been here for two weeks and he is showing the strain of the uncertainty."

"Do you think he is right?" Isobel pressed.

Maria averted her eyes. "I am not totally without hope," she said quietly, and then she moved away.

At dinner Isobel could not push her brooding thoughts aside. *Perhaps I was foolish to think anything I did here would matter.* She wondered if she should have told Davi about what she had overheard. He had said it wasn't her fault, but perhaps he was only being kind. Then she remembered his words about what would happen to them. He did not seem afraid to tell her what he really thought.

When the meal was nearly finished, Franco called the young people forward. Luis stumbled over his feet in his excitement and finally joined the others and held his berimbao ready. As the notes of the twangy, vibrating tune resonated into the evening, a hushed silence fell over the adults. Arms were slipped around shoulders, hands reached out to touch other hands, and even baby Rayna, who had been fussing ever since they arrived, gurgled contentedly in her mother's arms. The children played three tunes, and then Abraham Israel and his sons played several more.

This time Rachelle stood up. "Ever since we came here, Isobel has been trying to teach a few of us our letters. We're not the best students," she laughed, "but we have learned a few words. Can we show you?"

With encouragement from the group, Paulo handed Isobel the Bible, and she lined the children up in a row, feeling that all eyes were upon her. Although they read only a few words, and Isobel had to fill in often, each child showed how far he had come. Isobel read aloud for Paulo as he pointed to each word. " . . . And God divided the light from the darkness . . . "

The families hugged their children as they finished. Maria embraced Rachelle and Isobel together.

"I am filled with pride," she said, "as much for the student as for the teacher."

Davi leaned toward Isobel, his eyes cast down. "Remember when I offered to teach you the Hebrew prayers?" he asked. "I'd still like to do it."

Isobel smiled. "If you don't think it's useless," she teased, "I'd like to learn."

"I guess sometimes I speak before I think," he whispered. That was all he said, but Isobel understood.

She fell asleep that night with Davi's words in her mind and a sense of accomplishment that began to dispel her doubts. Perhaps she could not have prevented the first mate from carrying out his plan. And maybe she was beginning to make amends for her lack of trust. She slept a deep sleep that was not troubled by dreams of her sister, Maria, or of faraway places that she could not reach.

"Isobel! Isobel! Wake up!" Isobel awoke with a start and opened her eyes in darkness.

"What is it? she whispered. "What's wrong?"

Rachelle's voice was urgent. "Listen!"

At first Isobel heard only the sound of the others in the hut moving around in the darkness. She saw Asser's figure bend low and dash out the doorway. A loud crack and a thundering boom reached her ears. The air seemed to resonate with the sound.

Rachelle gripped her hand tightly. "It's cannons," she said. "At the harbor."

Paulo crawled over to the girls and Rachelle put her free arm around him, holding him close.

"What is happening?" Isobel asked, but Rachelle was as silent as Paulo.

Flashes of light from exploding cannons illuminated the sky like lightning bolts. Maria urged the children to the back of the hut, away from the doorway, and she and Rachel Nuñes planted themselves protectively in front of the cowering trio. They remained there, not talking or moving, for what seemed like hours.

Toward dawn, Asser and Davi returned to the hut. They seated themselves cross-legged, and Asser spoke softly and wearily.

"Another ship has attacked from the cove. We cannot determine its country, but it has taken the privateers by surprise and seems to dominate the battle."

Davi spoke up then, and Isobel thought she detected his anxiety in the rapid-fire account he gave. "Franco and I climbed to the top of the gate and no one stopped us. The guards must have fled. We wanted to jump over the top and free the bar, but Father forbade us. I know I could have done it, but . . . "

"No more about it!" Asser whispered hoarsely. "If you are injured, we cannot run anywhere, can we? And escaping into the sugar cane will not get us to Amsterdam! For once in your life, listen to advice!"

Davi did not dare another response in the face of his father's anger. Isobel had never seen him looking so overcome.

"Please do not blame Davi," Maria pleaded. "We are all so frustrated with our helplessness. He only wanted to find a way out."

Asser said nothing, but Isobel understood that Davi felt he must act, must try to help. His father could not be angry with him for that. She had not forgotten Davi's conviction that they would soon be in the hands of the Inquisition.

"What can we do?" Paulo's mother asked. "How can we wait here like a herd of docile sheep?"

"I know it seems as if we do nothing but wait," Asser said with resignation. "But we have thought of every possible alternative, and we see no way out. Our only choice is to try to escape through the village and put ourselves in the hands of the natives, but there is no reason to believe they would try to shelter us. The privateers make this cove a frequent stop, and the villagers cannot afford to anger them. It's simply out of the question."

"I have news," Abraham said, entering the hut. "Franco hoisted himself to the roof and has a clear view of the cove. The new ship does not appear to be a caravel, so perhaps it is neither Spanish nor Portuguese. Apparently it has overwhelmed the privateers, because they have raised their sails."

Silence hung in the air. "Listen," Isobel whispered. "The cannons have stopped."

For a brief moment no one moved. Then, as if a spell had been broken, they all headed for the doorway, emerging one by one into the breaking dawn. The other huts emptied, too, and everyone looked up expectantly at Franco.

Pieces of straw from the thatched roof clung to Franco's breeches and shirt like pins in a pincushion.

As the sun appeared behind him, the wisps of straw seemed to glow with their own yellow light.

He pointed excitedly toward the shore. "They're sailing! The caravel is sailing for the open sea!"

"Does the new ship show its colors?" Abraham asked.

"No, Father. I don't see a flag. But they are lowering their longboats. They are rowing for the cove!"

Asser now spoke authoritatively to the assembled group. "We have a few minutes before we will be discovered. Assemble your belongings quickly. Wrap the Torah carefully in the bedding. Children, fill every available jug with fresh water." No other words were necessary to urge them along.

Isobel was filling jugs when she heard the sound of marching footsteps and strange voices approaching the stockade. Each person turned to stare at the gate. Isobel reached for Rachelle's hand. "Dear God," she breathed, "Let them not be pirates."

A commanding voice barked orders, but the words were unintelligible. Isobel's heart raced as she heard the beam drop to the ground with a heavy thud. The gates creaked as they were slowly pulled open.

 Broken
Dreams

Twelve men, looking surprised to see the families assembled in the compound, stood in awkward silence. One of the sailors exclaimed, *"Bon Dieu! Qu'est-ce que nous avons ici?"*

Abraham's face broke into a smile. "They're French!" he beamed, slapping Asser on the back. "Thank the Lord! They're French!"

Abraham attempted to communicate with the sailors. One young crewman came forward and introduced himself in halting Spanish.

"We are from the French merchant ship, *Sainte Cathérine*. Who are you?"

Abraham hesitated before answering. Isobel struggled to follow the conversation.

"We are six families of Jews, twenty-three in number. We were forced to flee Recife, our home in Brazil, and were passengers aboard the Dutch ship, *The Valck*. We were taken captive by the Spanish privateers and imprisoned in this stockade. You must tell us where you are bound and petition your captain to take us with you."

As Isobel listened to the response, she heard the one word she was secretly praying for. "Amsterdam!" she exulted, hugging Rachelle tightly. "The French ship is on its way to Amsterdam!"

Davi put his hand on Isobel's shoulder. "Not Amsterdam, Isobel," he said with disappointment. "The ship is headed to *New* Amsterdam."

Davi's words hit Isobel like a bucket of cold water. Her back stiffened. "New Amsterdam? I thought there was only one Amsterdam."

"There is," he explained. "New Amsterdam is a Dutch colony in the Americas, and it is named for the city the colonists left. It will not bring us to our destination, but it will be a safe stopover."

Isobel slumped to the ground. Small pebbles pressed sharply into her knees, but she was barely aware of them. She shook her head in disbelief. "No matter how far I travel, or how hard I try, I only get farther away from my sister. I don't think I'll ever see her again."

Rachelle put her arm around her. "Don't be upset, Isobel. The privateers are gone! We're safe!"

Davi stood by, awkwardly shifting from one foot to the other. "You were right, Isobel. You believed all along that something would save us from the Inquisition. Don't give up now."

"We can't stay here," Abraham announced. "The sailors think some of the privateers are still on the island, and that their ship will return for them, and for us. The crew will help us move our things to the cove and then see about our passage. They won't remain for supplies now that they have had the encounter with the privateers. Pick up your belongings. And don't forget the water. It will be more important than we thought."

Rachelle helped Isobel to her feet and Isobel held her arm to steady herself. Her head felt as light as when she was pulled from under the longboat. She absently held the parcels that were given to her and walked woodenly down the path, not noticing the briars that leaned into her way and stuck to her dress as she brushed past.

Before, I believed that I would find Maria again, she thought. As long as we stayed here, there was hope. Now, I know where I am going, and it is not to Amsterdam. At the beach, she dropped her bundles onto the fine white sand and sat on a pile of folded bedding.

"These sailors are so nice," Rachelle chirped, plopping herself down next to Isobel. "What a difference from the privateers! Remember how one of them shoved me on the path when I couldn't keep up? These crewmen actually helped me! Did you know one of them carried all of Judica's bundles when he saw she was holding the baby?" Rachelle interrupted her own chattering and looked sympathetically at Isobel's impassive face. "Please cheer up," she pleaded. "We are going to be safe, and we are going to be together. Don't you always say that is the most important thing?"

Isobel could not bring herself to answer. Yes, she did think that was important. If she did not, she wouldn't have chosen to join the group when they left *The*

Valck. But there was something else in her life that was more important. She had to find her family. She knew now, more than ever before, how much she missed them. Why couldn't they make it to Amsterdam together so that she could reach her dream without giving up the closeness she had just found?

It is like my silver combs, she thought. If I wore one, and not the other, I would be out of balance. Maybe having no dream at all would be better than never being able to make it come true.

Isobel barely noticed when the longboats returned to shore, but when the captain of the ship began to address the group, she looked in his direction. The four Jewish men moved off with him, apparently to discuss the passage arrangements.

Davi flopped down on the sand and stretched his long, lanky body. He groaned loudly. "I'm so tired from carrying the baggage," he complained. "I can't move another muscle. It's a good thing we left your trunks on *The Valck*, Rachelle, or we would never have made it to the beach in less than a week."

Isobel tried not to listen as Davi and Rachelle argued about which items a person needed and which were unnecessary. Why do they always bicker about such unimportant things? She looked toward the ocean and stared fixedly at the French ship, riding gracefully at anchor. A change in Davi's tone caught her attention.

"I am relieved to be saved from the Inquisition, but I don't like the looks of this Captain Jacques de la Motthe," he was saying in a loud whisper. "Doesn't he have shifty eyes? See how he averts them when he talks to Papa and the others?"

Isobel noticed the captain was dressed in clothes that seemed too elegant for his post on a ship. His boots were of soft leather and gleamed in the sun. How had he managed to keep them dry? He wore a ruffled white shirt, and a fine cape flowed from his shoulders almost to his knees. The captain cut a lean figure; the bones above his eyes and at his cheeks protruded, giving his face a harsh, weathered look. She focused now on the captain's eyes. Davi was correct. His glance darted back and forth from the ground to the trees in the distance. Not once did he look forthrightly at anyone. It was as if his eyes might give away some private secret if he allowed anyone to gaze into them.

"I don't think the discussion of our passage is going smoothly," Davi announced. "Look at Abraham, how he shakes his head and gestures with his hands. He seems to protest. Now look at the captain's face. He is made of stone."

Davi seemed to have judged the situation accurately, although Rachelle immediately began to argue. The men seemed upset, and the captain looked smug. The faces of the four men were grim and resigned. Isobel exchanged a look of silent understanding with Davi as he stood up and headed to the group of adults to hear what had happened.

Rachelle tagged along. "You're wrong, Davi. Why don't you admit it for once? Papa's worked everything out and we're going to get away from here. Who cares what the captain's eyes look like?"

I thought Rachelle had changed, Isobel mused. In some ways she has, but not when it comes to Davi. There she goes, nattering away at him like a monkey, telling him he's completely wrong. Of course he can be just as stubborn, but he seems to have a better understanding of people. Maria would say he was *simpático*. I think you would like Davi, Maria, she communicated mentally. I wish you could know him.

Davi and Rachelle did not return before it was time to load the longboats and board the *Ste. Cathérine*. Isobel picked up as many bundles as she could carry and was rowed to the ship with David Israel Faro, his wife, Matilde, and their four children. David looked serious and preoccupied, staring out across the ocean. Matilde had a wide smile pressed on her face, whether out of satisfaction at getting underway, or to hide her own anxiety, Isobel was not sure. Marcella and Gracia sat politely, holding hands, while the older boys sat stiff and straight, looking at no one. Isobel was glad to be in their company, away from Rachelle's nervous chattering.

Once on deck, however, Isobel felt drawn to the Levys. She realized with a mixture of comfort and trepidation that she had come to think of that family as her own.

Rachelle wasted no time complaining about things. "I can't believe we have to leave more trunks behind! Mama says the captain would not take all of us *and* all our trunks, too. He swears he has a full hold and a large group of passengers already. He promised that another French ship will follow in just a day or two and that the natives will send along the rest. Do you think it's a good idea to trust those natives? What if they don't tell the next ship that we have left anything behind? Surely, no one would ever know the difference."

"It does sound risky," Isobel agreed absently.

Davi looked at Rachelle with annoyance. "If we were allowed passage only by leaving some of our things behind, what could we do? My paints and brushes and all my canvasses were left behind, too. How am I going to replace them? It's better to leave our belongings than to be left behind ourselves." He walked away before Rachelle could argue.

"We are to have space with the other passengers below deck, and can come up for fresh air whenever we choose," Rachelle announced.

Isobel thought of her confining space on the Dutch ship, as well as the imprisonment in the hold of the privateer. Which had been worse? At least when I was aboard *The Valck*, I was on my way to Amsterdam. Even when we were in Cuba, I had hope of finding Maria again. She looked searchingly at Rachelle. "Do you think it is better to have a dream that may not come true, or is it better not to have any dreams at all?"

Rachelle thought for a minute. "Do you mean big, important dreams, or just little wishes?" she asked.

Isobel was disappointed at the response. Perhaps she doesn't have any special dreams, at least not like mine. "Never mind," she said. She did not think she could explain what she meant to Rachelle. "It was a silly question."

Paulo made his way toward the girls, his face bright and eager. He stood in front of Isobel and reached his hand toward her. He was holding something.

"It's my Bible!" she exclaimed. "I forgot you had it."
The boy smiled proudly.

"Can we start our reading lessons again?" Rachelle
asked.

"I don't know," Isobel said. She felt no more interest
in reading. Or in planning for the future. Perhaps, she
thought, smaller dreams are best. Maybe making the
most of each day is all I can hope for. Maybe that is
enough. At least for now. She looked into Paulo's eager
face.

"All right," she agreed. "We'll start tomorrow morning."

The wind was brisk, the sails billowed, and the *Ste.
Cathérine* made good progress. The group carved out a
space among the other passengers with difficulty. The
ship was bigger than *The Valck*, but the captain had
not lied. It was already crowded with colonists heading
for the new land. The passengers were in such close
quarters that the captain forbade any cooking below
deck. Everyone was to be fed by the ship's cook. The
air smelled somewhat cleaner than on the Dutch ship,
and Isobel decided it was because the families were
not constantly preparing food.

Isobel and Rachelle settled down to sleep next to
each other, and Isobel tucked her Bible safely under
her folded dress. Well, Maria, you told me it would
keep me company when I was lonely. I didn't believe
you then, but I do now. It brought me closer to Paulo
and even to Rachelle. If I didn't have it, I couldn't teach
the children to read.

Maria Levy came to tuck them in and kiss them
goodnight. It was a ritual that had become more im-

portant to Isobel with each passing day. At first she felt uncertain of her right to be treated as part of the family and was worried about Rachelle's jealousy. But as the practice had developed into a routine, Rachelle accepted it and Isobel came to depend on it. No matter what happened during the day, she knew she could look forward to that comforting ending.

It was warm in the passenger quarters, but Maria squatted down next to Isobel and fussed at the blankets for a few moments before speaking in a barely audible voice. "I know you are troubled, child." The lanterns on the beams overhead flickered and their reflection glowed in Maria's eyes. "We will still be a long way from our destination. But at least we know where we are headed and we have reason to believe that everything will turn out right in the end." She smiled. "Won't the privateers be surprised to see that their bounty money has sailed over the horizon!"

Isobel remembered that Maria had said she was not totally without hope. Perhaps she knows about dreams. "Maria," she began softly, so that Rachelle could not hear, "do you think it is better to hold onto a dream that might not come true, or is it better to allow yourself no dreams at all?"

The woman reached for Isobel's hand and stroked it gently. "Who can know for certain if a dream will come true? That uncertainty is the nature of dreams." She gave Isobel an understanding look. "Some people are dreamers. Life has made them so. They have vast hopes and plans for their future, and that is what keeps them alive. Now, Davi, he is a dreamer. Maybe that is what gives him the gift of drawing things that many of us never notice. I know that is why he takes things so seriously. You see, when he suffers a setback, he thinks his dreams are shattered. I hope he is finally learning that all things that are broken can be put back together again, although they may not always be exactly the same as they were before. Rachelle, on the other hand, is not a dreamer. She takes life as it comes, and each day is an end in itself for her."

"But which way is better?"

"There is only one way for each of us. Just remember that sometimes, when we patch our broken dreams together, they look a little different than they did before they were broken. But, they still hold fast."

Isobel reached her arms around Maria and kissed her cheek. The ship rocked gently on the waves, lulling Isobel into sleepiness. Maria smoothed Isobel's hair and kissed her forehead. Isobel did not even notice when she moved away, for in a moment she was asleep.

Ship Bound

Isobel stood at the railing. Wisps of fog floated up toward the rising sun, and the ocean stretched as far as she could see. How far was New Amsterdam? How far away was Maria?

"Buenos días!" a voice greeted her. "You are one of the new passengers, no?"

"Sí, Señor," Isobel answered cautiously. She recognized the young French sailor as the volunteer who had addressed them in the stockade.

"You did not sleep well?" he asked, and Isobel responded in slow, clear Portuguese. Perhaps if I can understand his Spanish, he can also understand my language, she hoped.

"I got up early to watch the sun rise." She pointed to the horizon where pink and gray clouds hovered at the edge of the sky.

"Yo entiendo," replied the young man. "I understand. It is beautiful, no?" Isobel thought the sailor did

not look too much older than Davi. "I am Jean-Pierre Baptiste," he said with a polite bow.

"I am Isobel Ben Lazar," she responded. "I was traveling from Recife to Amsterdam to find my family."

"Such a young child has lost her family?" the sailor said in disbelief. "How could you have been so careless?" He laughed at what he seemed to think was a very funny joke, but when he saw that Isobel had not joined in his humor, he stopped. "Forgive me," he apologized. "Of course, this is not a matter to be taken lightly."

Isobel turned her back on the young man, gripping the polished railing firmly and again looking out to sea. The clouds opened into colors of purple and rose like a blossoming flower. What a fool, she thought, to make a joke of someone else's misfortune. And I'm not a child!

"*Pardón*," persisted the sailor apologetically. "*Lo siento mucho.*"

But Isobel would not waste any more words with him. Careless, indeed! Did he think she had lost her family as one misplaces a useless toy?

She heard his footsteps strike the deck and then fade. Perhaps she should have accepted his apology. She turned, but he was gone. Instead she saw Paulo ambling toward her, a smile on his face. I think the others are actually grateful to be on their way to New Amsterdam, Isobel thought. Am I the only one who is not content?

"Are we the only ones awake, then?" she asked, giving him an affectionate hug. Paulo shook his head and made a wide arc with his arms. "Everyone's up?"

she questioned him, and he nodded. "Well, then, we can meet here later for a reading lesson. Here, you keep the Bible so you can practice whenever you want."

The schedule was repeated each day as the ship cut through the water toward its destination. After a tasteless breakfast of stale biscuits and watery mush, the children sat with Isobel, practicing reading. In the afternoon, the berimbaos were brought out. Some of the sailors hung about, listening to the melodies and occasionally breaking into a lively jig. When the captain was out of earshot, their claps and shouts mixed with the music and floated across the deck.

Although I am doing all the same things I did on the island, Isobel thought, I do not feel as happy about them. She did not understand her lack of energy and the feeling that nothing seemed important or worthwhile. Rachelle's prattle bothered her and Paulo's continued silence seemed to hail her like a flag of surrender.

Isobel was startled from her worried thoughts one morning as she climbed on deck just as a sailor's boot struck the ladder from above. He muttered angrily, but then stepped aside when he realized that his obstacle was a girl. As Isobel emerged, she saw that it was the same young man she had encountered her first morning on the ship. Although she was sorry for the way she had acted, she had not dared to approach him to apologize. She did not know how to excuse her rudeness.

The sailor looked as flustered at meeting her as she did at running into him. At the same time, they each blurted out, *"Pardón!"* A cautious grin spread across his face, and in a moment they were both laughing at the memory of their first encounter.

He took her elbow and guided her to the railing. The waves splashed against the ship and sprayed a fine mist into the air.

"At the risk of opening a sore wound," Jean-Pierre Baptiste began, "I would be honored if you would tell me how you have become separated from your parents. To make amends for my 'faux pas,' perhaps I can assist you in finding them again."

"I wish someone could help me," Isobel said, explaining how she had come to be aboard the *Ste. Cathérine.* "But, you see, my only hope for finding my family is to get to Amsterdam."

"You are much more courageous than most young girls," Jean-Pierre said sincerely. "It is important that you accept what has happened. We cannot change life if we sit crying over it."

Isobel thought about the sailor's words. Davi told me that change is what makes us grow, but he meant changes we cannot control. Jean-Pierre means the changes that we make for ourselves. So many people have advice to give me, but still, all I have are dreams.

"There is a possibility of reaching your destination," the sailor said.

Isobel caught her breath. "How?" she asked quickly. "I thought this ship would only sail to New Amsterdam."

"The cargo on board is destined for the colony, but in turn, we will take pelts and tobacco to Amsterdam for the Dutch West India Company. The problem would be raising passage money. The Jews are already indebted to the captian for the fare to New Amsterdam."

Isobel remembered her silver combs. Maria had told her that, if necessary, they could be sold. They would surely be worth enough to pay passage. But could she bring herself to part with them?

"There is another problem," she admitted. "One I have created myself. I do not think I could bear to leave the Levys. They are like a family to me now."

"Why do you assume you would have to part? Don't they, too, wish to reach Amsterdam?" He shrugged his shoulders and his hands spread in thc air. "You see, it is only a matter of the fare."

Isobel's heart raced. Would her combs be valuable enough to provide passage for them all? In her excitement, she nearly told Jcan-Pierre about her hidden treasure, but caught herself in time. Do not worry, Maria, she mentally reassured her sister. I will not risk losing the combs. At least, not before I must. I haven't even told Maria Levy about them. Perhaps it is time that I did.

But then she thought of another reason to keep her secret to herself. What if the group needed the combs to help pay for the fare to New Amsterdam? Then she would lose her last link to her family and her only hope of reaching her destination. She could not risk that, even if it meant hiding them selfishly.

"Jean-Pierre," she asked. "Did you say the Jews were indebted to Captain de la Motthe?"

"*Sí, es verdad.* It's true." He lowered his voice and inclined his head closer to Isobel. "The captain has negotiated the passage of the Jews for *mucho, mucho dinero*. Much money." He spoke with a note of anger.

"More than it should cost?" she asked.

"*Sí,*" Jean-Pierre answered, holding his finger to his lips as an unspoken warning not to repeat his confidence. "But, of course, the captain has his reasons." The sailor counted them out on his fingers for emphasis. "First, the ship is already crowded and the extra passengers have overloaded us and slowed us down. Second, you must all be provided with food and our supplies are dangerously low. Third," he looked at Isobel apologetically, "the captain does not wish to become involved with Jews."

Isobel grew defensive. "Then why did he take us at all? He could have left us in Cuba."

The sailor rubbed his thumb across his remaining fingers. "*Dinero. Mucho dinero.*"

"But nearly everything was taken from us," Isobel protested. "The captain cannot take our money if we have none."

Jean-Pierre shook his head. "Not true," he explained. "The captain is shrewd. He has drawn up a contract which your friends have signed. Only a portion of the amount has been paid, but he knows they have connections in Amsterdam, and that they will get the money somehow. Now you see why I say the only problem is raising the money to pay your fare. So do not worry yet. Your friends may surprise you with their resources."

Isobel felt as if a heavy burden had been lifted. She had kept her hopes alive when she was in the stockade in Cuba. Now that they were free of the Inquisition and on their way to a safe port, there was new reason to be hopeful. Perhaps Maria Levy was right, she thought, and my dreams have been patched together. They may look different than in their original form, but they are holding together, nonetheless.

Isobel began enjoying life on board. She was no longer afraid to reach out and hug Maria. Each time she felt the woman's arms around her, she was sure she had made the right decision when she chose to join the group. She talked often with Rachelle, and they were becoming friends. Rachelle was teaching her to embroider with needle and thread she borrowed from one of the passengers.

The days filled with activity, but Isobel especially looked forward to Friday nights. In the glow of the Shabbat candles, Davi began teaching her the Hebrew prayers. Isobel was fascinated with the musical flow of the new language.

Even Jean-Pierre found time to mingle with them in between his duties on the ship, and soon the whole group relished his shipboard gossip and developed a taste for his wry humor.

One evening he teasingly offered them an important piece of news. "The children must guess what I have seen today, and if they can rightly name it, the news it portends will be worth the effort!"

"Was it on the ship, or off the ship?" Davi asked.

"Both!"

There was a moment of puzzled silence. "Was it bigger than baby Rayna?" asked Estrella.

"*Sí!* It was bigger, but also smaller!"

"Does it have legs, or does it float?" asked Franco scientifically.

"Both!"

Isobel was confused. "If it was on the ship and off the ship, big and small, with legs and also floating, then there must be more than one thing. Is that right?"

"*Sí!*"

Paulo stepped forward eagerly and tugged Jean-Pierre's sleeve for attention. "Yes, Paulo. Do you have a guess?"

The boy nodded and his eyes gleamed as he proceeded to act out his guess. He squatted down on the deck and tucked his hands under his armpits. For a moment, he pretended to sway with the rhythm of the ship, and then he spread his arms, flapping them wildly, as he stood and moved around the group, pretending to be looking down from a great height.

"*Bravo!*" said Jean-Pierre, applauding him.

"It's a duck!" Rachelle shouted. "No! It's a seagull! A seagull! We're coming to land!"

A cheer rose from the passengers as the news was passed among them. "Land!" they shouted, embracing each other with enthusiasm.

"It's New Amsterdam," Jean-Pierre announced. "We shall arrive in port in about three days."

Franco and Avram began playing a bouncy tune, and Paulo and Jean-Pierre danced a little jig. There was reason to celebrate. The long journey was nearly over.

"What will it be like?" Rachelle asked her mother that night. "Is it cold in New Amsterdam? Will they be glad to see new people? Will we stay long?"

"It is autumn in the colony, but it is not yet too

cold. It will be very cold, they say, if we stay through the winter, and we may have to, as there will be few ships starting across the ocean after September. We hope the colonists will be hospitable to us, but their governor, Peter Stuyvesant, is not a tolerant man. We will see what our welcome is and then determine how long we stay."

"The *Ste. Cathérine* will sail to Amsterdam after it takes on new cargo," Isobel said hesitantly. "Maybe we could work for our passage."

"You forget that there are twenty-three of us. And we already owe Captain de la Motthe more than we can pay. But do not worry about it, child. God has looked out for us up until now. He will provide."

That night, Isobel's sleep was filled with the dream of the moss-covered castle that had recurred so often. Usually, Isobel searched through the grass in vain, trying to find where her silver combs had fallen, but that night the dream changed in one aspect. As Isobel searched through the deep meadow grasses for her combs, she found them. Only they were broken in pieces.

First one jagged piece of silver pinched her hand. "Maria!" she called after her sister. "Here they are! Help me put them back together!" But Maria did not turn, and as in all the other dreams, she did not answer. More pieces of the broken comb jabbed at Isobel's fingers, and soon she held a small pile of broken fragments. It was a puzzle she could not piece together.

"Maria!" she screamed in desperation. But there was no answer.

 The Shores
of New
Amsterdam

Isobel pushed against the ship's railing with
the other passengers, waiting for her first glimpse of
the new colony. Seagulls glided effortlessly around
them and their shrill cries announced the ship's approach. She clutched Davi with one hand and Rachelle
with the other.

Davi took a deep breath. "Well, here comes one more
change," he said. He reached over and tugged playfully
at Isobel's hair. In just the space of a few weeks it had
grown longer and the blunt ends left by Cado's knife
had softened into natural waves. "I told you it would
make your hair grow."

"I never expected what was ahead when I first left

the monastery," Isobel said. She could make out the green of treetops and the outline of the shore as the ship sailed toward the harbor. Her head was filled with the memories of all that had happened to her since she stood holding Maria's hand at her first sight of Recife. "I barely escaped from the church, you know, because one of the friars caught me just as I was getting onto *The Valck*. I don't know how I convinced him to let me go. It seems like such a long time ago."

Davi looked surprised. "But the hardest part wasn't escaping," he said. "It was choosing to come with us when we were captured."

Rachelle squeezed her hand. "I'm glad you came. I can hardly remember when you weren't here. It's already September," she said. "Mama says it's nearly Rosh Hashonah. It's a new year, a new land, and a new life in New Amsterdam!"

"The harbor looks so calm," Davi said. "I hope our reception is as peaceful as the water. Governor Stuyvesant doesn't like settlers of different faiths."

Rachelle broke in. "Jean-Pierre told me that the governor has already refused permission for a group of Lutherans and some Quakers to establish churches here. I don't think that he will welcome Jews."

For once, Davi did not argue. "Still," he said, "we will have to stay at least through the winter, since it will take that long to pay off the debt to Captain de la Motthe and earn enough to book passage on another ship." Isobel hoped that a way would be found to go to Amsterdam when the *Ste. Cathérine* sailed. She still had her combs.

"For all twenty-three of us," Davi said, "we were charged 2,500 guilders. We have already paid about 900 guilders, although Papa would not tell me where it came from."

"How will we pay the rest?" Isobel asked, concern evident in her voice.

"If our belongings arrive from Cuba," Davi answered, "there are things we could sell. Like Abraham's berimbaos. And my paints. There is another possibility. Mose says several Dutch Jews are involved with the Dutch West India Company and we could arrange the captain's payment through them when he arrives."

Isobel looked down at the small bundle of blankets at her feet. Some bedding and a collection of cooking pots were all the captain was permitting the Jews to carry ashore. Their few remaining trunks and possessions, including their clothes, had to be left on board as a guarantee of payment. Davi said that was just like ransom, making the families pay to get their own things back. But Mose Lumbrusco had argued successfully for the Torah scroll. Since the captain considered it worthless, he had agreed.

Behind her, Isobel heard the clanking of iron chains as the heavy anchor was lowered into the water. Several crewmen prepared the rowboats to bring the passengers ashore. Bundles were lowered over the side and then each passenger climbed unsteadily down a rope ladder into the narrow, rocking longboat. Isobel sat nervously with the Levys and the Nuñes family. The oars sliced through the water and the settlement came into clearer view.

The colony seemed smaller than Recife, but the

streets were laid out in a similar cluster of rows, all facing the harbor. People lined the shore and bright handkerchiefs waved in the air. The billowing sails of a windmill turned slowly in a farmyard.

"Is that a stockade on the outskirts?" Rachelle asked. "They won't shut us up as prisoners, will they?"

"I don't expect so," Asser said. "Governor Stuyvesant may not wish us to establish a permanent residence here, but this is a Dutch colony and he should not persecute us. The stockade is probably built for protection from Indians in the unsettled lands to the north."

"Indians?" Rachelle said with a puzzled look. "Aren't they friendly, like in Recife?"

"I certainly hope so."

"Well, where will we stay, then?" Rachelle demanded.

"Stop worrying, Rachelle, and stop chattering."

Rachelle fell silent at her father's mild rebuke. Rachelle did sometimes go on until it was hard to listen to her, but it wasn't a serious fault, and today Isobel shared the questions she had asked.

Gravel scraped the bottom of the longboats as they glided onto the shore, and the passengers set their feet on land once again. Relatives and acquaintances rushed forward, and there were shouts of joy as families and friends were reunited. Jean-Pierre lifted Isobel lightly from the boat and set her down on the dry, sandy beach.

"Good luck!" he called, as he headed toward the village, his belongings piled in a sack. "I'll be back!" Sailors unloaded trunks and baggage and the colonists carried them away. The harbor emptied of people, the longboats were rowed back to the ship, and soon only the band of Jews were left standing alone on the shore.

The captain approached and ordered them to appoint one member to accompany him to the governor's house. There, he said, they would explain the circumstances of their arrival and their great debt. Because of his fluency in languages, Abraham was selected. The rest spread out blankets and waited in the sun. The older boys sat together on the sand and the younger children huddled close to their parents. Davi's sketch book was propped on his lap, but the charcoal lay unused beside him. Isobel sat between Asser and Maria, wondering what news Abraham would bring.

For a time, no one spoke. Then Paulo wiggled in next to Isobel and removed a small object from his doublet. Although the sailors had strict orders to search the Jews for any valuable items they might try to remove from the ship, the sailors had winked at the children and passed them by. What had Paulo managed to carry out?

"You've still got the Bible!" Isobel remembered.

Paulo opened the book to the final pages and showed Isobel what he had found. "Why, it's Psalms," she said. "I didn't even know they were there. I see you have been practicing reading on your own, Paulo, and have made good use of the book." She gave the boy a hug.

Paulo pushed the book at her again and the afternoon breeze ruffled the pages. "This isn't a good time to read," she said quietly. "Everyone is too tired."

Paulo shook his head in disagreement and pointed to a specific passage.

"Go ahead," Maria said. "It would be comforting to have you read, Isobel. Maybe we should hear about Jonah and the whale," she smiled. "We certainly have been swallowed up and spit out on shore enough times." Asser chuckled. Isobel looked at the passage Paulo pointed out. It was Psalm 18, but Isobel had never noticed it before. "I guess Paulo wants this passage," she said to Maria. She began to read softly. The others turned toward her and listened.

"The sorrows of death compassed me, and the floods of ungodly men made me afraid." She noticed that the corner of the page was bent and that a small smudge of dirt showed where Paulo had thumbed it. He must have read this passage through many times, she thought. I didn't realize he could read so well. But how could I? He never read out loud.

"In my distress I called upon the Lord, and cried unto my God; out of His temple He heard my voice, and my cry came before Him into His ears." Do I finally trust in God, like this? she questioned herself.

Then Paulo reached over and lifted the book from her hand. Isobel was confused. Did he want her to stop? Wasn't she reading the passage he had asked for?

In a shaky hesitant voice, Paulo began to read aloud: "He sent from on high, He took me, He drew me out of many waters. He delivered me from mine enemy most strong, and from them that hated me: for they were too mighty for me."

Tears welled up in Isobel's eyes as she heard Paulo's timid voice. Rachel Nuñes rose up from her seat and gave a soft, sharp cry. She covered her face with her hands. A murmur stirred the group and all eyes were upon the boy. But Paulo ignored them all, serene in his achievement. His words became stronger, and he continued to the end of the passage.

"They confronted me in the day of my calamity: but the Lord was a stay unto me. He brought me forth also into a large place; He delivered me, because He delighted in me." He closed the book and handed it to Isobel.

"No, Paulo," she said. "It's yours. I think it was always meant for you."

Rachel engulfed Paulo in her arms, her audible sobs a release of emotions that had been stored far too long. "Paulo, *filho*," she said softly. "My child."

Isobel felt her heart would burst with sadness at what Paulo had gone through, and with joy at what had occurred.

"You have a hand in this," Asser said. "By teaching Paulo to read, you gave him the chance to break his silence without having to find words for his own thoughts. I think he has let the Psalm speak for him."

We have all come out of many waters, Isobel thought. Paulo picked the right message. We are safe upon the shore. Although it's not the one I dreamed of, it is the one I have chosen.

Hand in hand, Paulo and his mother walked along the water's edge as Paulo spoke quietly to her.

Abraham returned just then, but even his news seemed less important than what had just happened.

"This Stuyvesant is a difficult man," Abraham was saying. "He wants us to settle our debt with de la

Motthe and go on to Amsterdam." Isobel wondered if there was a chance that they might sail with the *Ste. Cathérine*.

"How does he expect us to pay what we owe, let alone raise more money for another passage?" Sultana asked.

"He has no sympathy for the exorbitant charge, nor for what has happened to us," Abraham explained. "I tried to explain that we have already paid full fare for our passage on *The Valck*, and have lost everything of value to the privateers. But the governor turns his head as if he were deaf."

"How much time do we have?" Mose asked.

"He has granted us one week to settle the debt, but he will not allow us to remove our tools and clothes from the *Ste. Cathérine*. And the captain refuses to wait until we petition our friends in Holland for the sum."

Isobel listened closely. They had no way to make enough money to pay de la Motthe in one week, even if their trunks did arrive.

"There is one piece of information I learned that may be helpful," Abraham added. "It seems there are two other Jews here in New Amsterdam. Jacob Bar-Simon is a Dutchman who has been living here for about a year, and there is a merchant named Solomon Pietersen. I strongly suggest we search them out and try to enlist their help."

"That is a good idea," said Judica. "Someone should find them while we are free to move about the colony, and the rest of us will prepare a shelter for the night."

"If Abraham does not mind being called upon

again," Asser said, "I think he is our best spokesman. Does anyone wish to accompany him?"

"If these men are merchants," said Mose Lumbrusco, "I might be able to offer my services to them. In any case, I would like to make their acquaintance."

As the men headed off toward the town, Asser called after them. "And find out if they need a nice, kosher butcher," he said in mock seriousness. "My prices are reasonable!"

 Out of Many Waters

Rachelle sniffled and put her hand to her forehead. "I think I am becoming feverish," she complained. "This place does not agree with me. It is so cold and damp."

The families had made camp in a clearing of pine trees not far from the beach, where a fresh-water stream flowed toward the ocean and provided water for drinking, cooking, and washing. They had piled pine needles under their bedding for protection from the cold ground, but still they shivered through the night.

"We're all sniffling," Isobel said. "Even though it hasn't rained, by morning everything is wet."

Davi shook the brown pine needles from the blankets and draped them over branches to dry. "We've been camped here over a week, and there is still no sign of the second French ship. I wondered why de la Motthe was so anxious to be paid. Now I think it's because he knew our belongings would never come."

"I'll bet there never was another ship following the *Ste. Cathérine.*" Rachelle said, wiping her nose with a leaf. "I don't even have a handkerchief! It was just an excuse to leave our trunks and keep us from protesting too much."

The captain brought the matter of the debt to the attention of the colony's court, arguing to have it settled or the passengers put in jail. But the judges were sympathetic to the Jews and granted numerous extensions. The latest reprieve gave them three more days. "What will happen if our things do not arrive?" Isobel asked.

"The court will let the captain auction our remaining belongings until the full sum is raised," Davi explained. "I've seen it done in Recife. An item is held up before a crowd of people. If someone is interested, they call out how much they're willing to pay. Other people may call out higher amounts. The person who makes the highest offer purchases the item. In our case, the captain will keep the money toward what we owe."

"But we don't have much left," Rachelle said, "some clothes and blankets, a few tools and pots." She paused and then asked, "What if the auction doesn't raise enough?"

"De la Motthe has asked the court to put the men in jail until he gets his money." Davi looked worried.

"But that could take months," Isobel said. "And without the men to work, it could take years!" Davi nodded solemnly. "Is it possible," she asked, "that one item could raise so much money that the debt might be paid off right away? Then we wouldn't have to lose everything."

"If we had anything worth that much we would pay the captain. Do you think we want to be stuck here, camping in the cold, and making spectacles of ourselves in front of the entire colony?"

"Solomon Pietersen told Papa that the people are divided over whether or not we should be allowed to remain," Rachelle said importantly. "It seems we are the talk of the village."

Franco added his news. "Some of the folk say we should be welcomed in the spirit of tolerance and freedom," he said. "But others side with Governor Stuyvesant and say we will drain the charity of the colony."

"At least we are providing entertainment," Davi said sarcastically. He launched into a little jig, hopping lightly around the clearing and whistling a tune. Davi danced around faster and reached for Isobel's arm, pulling her toward him. The other children crowded around, laughing and pointing.

"What's gotten into you?" Isobel protested. But he only swung her around faster, nearly tripping over her feet.

At the end of his performance, he made a deep, exaggerated bow and flashed a big, artificial grin. Isobel leaned against a thick pine tree, laughing and trying to catch her breath. Davi walked around the clearing, holding his hat out in supplication. The children giggled and dropped pebbles into it.

"Don't act like a fool!" Rachelle scolded him.

"It's quite wise," Davi retorted. "In fact, it's the

solution to our problems. After all, entertainers should be paid for their work. Since we are providing such diversion for the good townfolk, let us pass the hat and receive our just rewards!"

"Come, children," said Maria. She dumped the stones out of Davi's hat and plunked it back on his head. "No more clowning. Tonight is Shabbat, and it is also Rosh Hashonah eve, the beginning of the holy days of the New Year. Jacob BarSimon and Solomon Pietersen will be joining us. They may even bring some chickens for a holiday feast."

"Why, I believe I've forgotten what a chicken tastes like," Davi exclaimed. He rubbed his hands together in anticipation. "Oh, for a juicy, roasted, browned, delicate morsel of chicken!"

"Today I met a boy from the village," Paulo said, "and he showed me some red fruit called apples. We can pick some for dinner."

Isobel was delighted every time Paulo spoke. He had resumed talking in a natural manner, though he was still shy. The change in him was enormous and he was more at ease now. He stood up tall and had an energetic bounce to his walk.

"Apples!" Paulo said, as if savoring the word. "Off we go for apples!"

Isobel and Rachelle bathed in the stream. They scrubbed their collars and cuffs and set them in the sun to dry, then helped prepare dinner. Everyone worked together closely, and by sundown, three plump chickens roasted over the fire, their dripping juices sizzling as they hit the flames. The aroma filled the camp.

Jacob BarSimon arrived, saying he wished he were more prosperous and able to offer his fellow Jews shelter or money to ease their situation. He was a young man with a gentle face and long black hair. He humbly offered two slim candles to be lit in honor of the holiday, and a small crock of honey.

"It is all I could spare," he apologized, "but I can assure you that eating apples and honey on Rosh Hashonah will guarantee a sweet year."

"Honey!" Abraham marvelled, raising the jar high in the air. "I feel that great things are about to happen!"

Solomon Pietersen, a middle-aged man with graying hair, had arrived earlier with the chickens dangling limply in his hands. A few pin feathers stuck to his coat. He was a respected merchant, but like Jacob, he rented a small room and had little to spare. Still, he knew the laws of the colony and was invaluable in speaking to the court on behalf of the Jews. Asser felt they owed their continued freedom to him.

The beautiful embroidered tablecloth and the polished brass candlesticks had been held on the ship, but Sultana and Maria fixed the candles to a tree stump and decorated it with wildflowers and brightly colored leaves and grasses.

Asser Levy began to speak in his quiet, yet commanding, voice. He did not have to ask for silence. That came of its own accord. Isobel listened to him with respect.

"We gather tonight to welcome the Sabbath Queen and the New Year. Rosh Hashonah is a period of reflection, a time to ask God to forgive our failings and inscribe us for a good year to come."

Isobel caught Davi's eye. He was mouthing a word silently. She studied his face. He was saying "forgive." She felt her face grow warm. Isobel could ask for forgiveness for not telling the others about the plan.

"We have spent the day in busy activity," Asser went on, "but the real preparation for the New Year must come from within our deepest selves. We must put our transgressions behind us and look to a new beginning."

Rachel Nuñes stepped to the makeshift table. "I have been asked to say the blessing over the candles," she said, "in recognition of God's blessing on my son. But, I would like to ask Isobel to kindle the flame and to recite the prayer with me. She has done more than I can express in becoming part of each of us."

Isobel's throat felt choked with emotions. She stepped forward hesitantly. She had heard the prayer so many times now, and practiced it over and over with Davi's patient help, but did she know it well enough to recite it in front of everyone? She looked from face to face and felt as if a special warmth flowed from each person around her. Maria nodded her encouragement.

She took the taper from Rachel and touched it to the candlewicks. The flames flickered in the breeze and then took hold.

"*Baruch atoh adonai,*" she began, closing her eyes and pulling the glow of the candles toward her. All else was shut out. The voice of Rachel Nuñes blended with her own, and the prayer rolled off her lips. At its conclusion, Rachel embraced her tightly.

"*Shabbat shalom,* Rachel," Isobel said.

The rest of the blessings were recited and the apples

and honey were passed around, to Paulo's special delight.

Davi came up to Isobel. "Happy New Year," he said. "I have something for you." He held a piece of paper out to her and Isobel saw that it was one of his sketches. The soft, fuzzy lines of charcoal showed a group of children looking up at an older girl who was holding a book out to them. The girl's face concentrated on the children, but there was a glow about her. She seemed kind and filled with love. A shock of recognition came over her and Isobel became flustered. She turned to Davi. "Is it . . . is it . . . me?"

He smiled at her. "Don't you know?"

Isobel realized that she had never seen her own reflection. There were no looking glasses at the monastery. She had never before seen her own face.

"It's beautiful, Davi." She couldn't think of anything to say that could possibly express her feelings.

Isobel slept that night unaware of the cold ground and with a peacefulness she had never enjoyed before. Even so, her old dream returned to haunt her. This time she knelt in front of the tree stump that held the Shabbat candles and searched in the dirt for her combs. The glowing flames lit the ground and illuminated the moss-covered castle in the distance.

"Help me, Maria," she said to her sister. "I must find the combs."

"Here they are," her sister said. She handed her two shiny objects, but they did not look like her silver combs.

"These aren't the same," she argued.

Her sister stood up and took Isobel's hand. "It

doesn't matter, *pequena irmã*. You don't need them anymore." She walked toward the castle, pulling Isobel along. It grew darker as they left the clearing, but Isobel heard the sound of trumpeters on the castle wall. Maria opened a thick wooden door and urged Isobel to enter. When Isobel stepped toward the threshold, Maria disappeared into the darkness.

"Maria!" she called after her. "Maria! Where are you?"

"I am here, child," came a voice from above. Isobel looked up and saw Maria Levy smiling down at her from the balcony. Asser and Rachelle and Davi were by her side. "Come," she called softly. "We are waiting for you."

When Isobel awoke, she could not forget the dream. She moved through her tasks that morning lost in thought.

It was the second day of Rosh Hashonah, and the group gathered at the edge of the shore for a final ceremony. Judica handed each of them a small crust of bread saved from the evening meal. Isobel felt the dry bread against her palm and remembered reaching for the bread Paulo had left her when she was hiding on *The Valck*.

"We cast small crumbs of bread onto the waves," Abraham explained, "as a symbol of throwing our transgressions and our sadnesses of the past year onto the waters. With the release of these crumbs, we cleanse our souls in preparation for a new beginning." With a flurry of hands in the air, the crumbs flew lightly onto the water. Isobel opened her fingers and released the bread. She was ready to cast her past upon the waves.

Although she felt a deep change within her, Isobel was sharply aware that the circumstances of the group had not changed. The second French ship, if there ever was one, never arrived, and Captain de la Motthe pursued the group's debt relentlessly. The court ordered the remaining goods to be auctioned.

"I'm sorry my trunks were lost," Rachelle sighed. "Maybe someone would have bought those stomachers I worked so hard to embroider."

Isobel watched warily as an early crowd of colonists assembled at the shore to see what items might be of use to them. "They'll want the pots and utensils," Mose declared. "Anything they can't make here."

"And the fabric," Rachel Nuñes added. "Good cloth is hard to come by."

Captain de la Motthe stood on the beach watching the proceedings while a representative of the court assembled the items to be sold. Jean-Pierre Baptiste approached the Jews. "I am sorry for what has happened," he said. Isobel smiled at him. She was glad she had forgiven the young man for his joke about her family and that she had apologized for her rudeness. She would not want to start the New Year with such a foolish deed on her conscience.

"Jean-Pierre," she whispered, "I must talk to you for a moment." They slipped away from the others, standing close to the water.

She handed the sailor a folded piece of paper. "Solomon Pietersen has gotten me paper and ink," she said, "and I have written to my sister, telling her where I am and letting her know that I am safe. Look," she said, pointing to the outside of the folded message, "I have written my sister's name and my parents' names here. When you get to Amsterdam, will you try to find them?"

"But, I thought you were to travel to Amsterdam with us," he protested. "I was sure you could raise the money. Perhaps today, after the auction, it will still be possible."

"No," Isobel said, shaking her head. "The debt is too great. And I must stay here, at least for now. You see, this is the only family that I know I have. It won't end my dream of finding Maria and my parents, it will just change it. Maybe, in the spring, we will all go to Amsterdam together. Or, maybe you will find my family and they will come here. You see, there is still hope."

The auction had begun and items were held aloft to the shouted bids of the colonists. The affair was quieter than Isobel had expected, and there seemed to be few competitors. "Will you take my letter?" she asked again.

"Of course," the young man assured her. "I promised I would find a way to help you. When I return next year, I will have news."

Isobel took Jean-Pierre's hand in hers. "Thank you," she said. "I will wait."

She walked to the man directing the sale and waited until he looked down at her. He questioned her in Dutch, but Isobel did not need to understand his words. She reached up and handed him something, gesturing toward the group.

A look of surprise registered on the man's ruddy face. He spoke with great excitement, and then held the items aloft for all to see. A murmur spread through the crowd as two small, silver filigreed combs were presented for bids.

Isobel walked back, her head erect, and a forced smile on her face. Maria rushed up to her, and held her close. "Oh, child," she said, tears forming in her eyes, "not your combs! Don't give them your combs!"

Isobel began to sob. The smile faded from her face and she dissolved in tears. Maria had known all along about the combs hidden in her chemise and had never said anything. Rachelle came and put her hand on Isobel's back, patting it soothingly.

Isobel tried to compose herself. She did not want to cry. She had done what she wanted to do. No one had forced her. No one had even asked her. It had been her choice to give up the combs to help pay off the debt.

In her blurred vision, she saw a stout woman advance to the auctioneer, pay the winning price, and walk off with them. I am sorry, Maria, she thought. Please forgive me, but I had to do it. You said they could be sold if that was the only way. It is the only way. I have more to think about now than myself.

The colonist ambled toward the group, her stiff apron and starched collar unmoved by the breeze. She stopped directly in front of Isobel and a soft, kind smile grew on her face. She held the combs in her outstretched hands. Isobel was confused. What did the woman want? She explained something in Dutch.

"She has bought them for you," Abraham translated. "She says they are a gift."

Isobel reached forward hesitantly, feeling the cool silver combs nestle into her palms.

The generous woman had set an example, and in a moment, other colonists walked to the Jews. They handed back the goods that had been theirs, although the settlers had spent their own precious guilders to obtain each item.

"I believe we have been accepted," Asser said. "We have much to offer this new land. We will stay."

That evening, Isobel stood on the shore and watched the *Ste. Cathérine* raise its sails. The silver combs gleamed in her hair, but tonight there were no tears glistening in her eyes. She had chosen. Her letter to her sister was cast upon the waters like the crumbs of bread she had scattered on Rosh Hashonah. Like Paulo, she had come out of many waters to a new shore and a new life.

Maybe, Maria, she thought, maybe you, too, have found a family. I hope and pray that you are not alone. We may still find each other someday. Waters shift with the tides, you know, and sometimes even crumbs cast upon the waves return to shore.

Afterword

You will not find Isobel Ben Lazar listed in early accounts of America's first immigrants, for she is a fictional character. Yet her story reflects the actual journey of twenty-three Jewish refugees who fled the shores of Recife, Brazil, in the 1600s. They landed in the colony of New Amsterdam after their ship was separated from a larger fleet and captured by Spanish privateers.

Although Isobel's character is imaginary, it is true that many Jewish children were taken from their families and sent to monasteries in remote colonies so they could be raised in the Catholic faith without interference. They were fed poorly and made to work long hours at difficult labor. Scores of these children died of malnutrition and tropical diseases. But some, like Isobel, survived.

Early New Amsterdam records confirm that twenty-three Jews arrived in the colony in September, 1654, aboard the French ship, the *Saint Cathérine*. In the group were Asser and Maria Levy, Rachel Nuñes, Judica de Mereda, Mose Lumbrusco, David Israel Faro, and Abraham Israel de Piza. The feelings of the colo-

198

nists toward these new arrivals varied. An angry letter written by a Reverend John Megapolensis urges that the Jews be sent away and calls them "godless rascals, who are of no benefit to the country." But the majority of colonists were kind and open-minded. Many offered food, and the Dutch Reformed Church gave them enough money to tide them over the winter.

By the end of their first year in New Amsterdam, the Jews had established themselves as part of the colony. They won the right to serve in the militia, hold office, and own land. Asser Levy became the first Jewish landowner in the colony, and with property he donated, the group built the first synagogue in the new land. They named their congregation "Shearith Israel," which means "Remnant of Israel." Although the original building did not survive the centuries, there is today a large and thriving temple in New York City, still called by the same name.

The French ship, the *Saint Cathérine*, is often called the Jewish *Mayflower*. Like the early Pilgrims, this small band of Jews set out across the ocean in search of religious freedom. They came to New Amsterdam by chance, as their Pilgrim counterparts arrived in Plymouth. They suffered great hardships in order to survive and prosper. As the Indians helped the Pilgrims over their first harsh winter, the Dutch colonists extended the hand of friendship to help the Jewish settlers. With courage, they grew in numbers and in strength, becoming one of the foundation blocks upon which the young country was built.

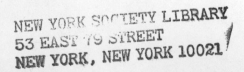

BIBLIOGRAPHY

Baker, William A., *Colonial Vessels*, Massachusetts: Barre Publishing, 1962.

Dubin, Rabbi Maxwell H., *Jews in American History*, Los Angeles, The Wilshire Boulevard Temple, 1930.

Eban, Abba, *Heritage: Civilization and the Jews*, New York: Summit Books, 1984.

Friedman, Lee M., *Early American Jews*, Cambridge, MA: Harvard University Press, 1934.

Marcus, Jacob, *The Colonial American Jew*, Detroit: Wayne State University Press, 1970.

Marcuse, Sibyl, *A Survey of Musical Instruments*, New York: Harper and Row, 1975.

Marcuse, Sibyl, *Musical Instruments*, New York: W. W. Norton, 1975.

Pessin, Deborah, *History of the Jews in America*, New York: Abelard-Schuman, 1957.

Wilcox, R. Turner, *Five Centuries of American Costume*, New York: Scribner's and Sons, 1963.

Wiznitzer, Arnold, *Jews in Colonial Brazil*, New York: Columbia University Press, 1960.

Wiznitzer, Arnold, *The Number of Jews in Dutch Brazil*, New York: Jewish Social Status, Vol. 16 #2, 1954.

Wiznitzer, Arnold, *Records of the Earliest Jewish Communities in The New World*, New York: American Jewish Historical Society, 1954.

Worrell, Estelle Ansley, *Children's Costumes in America, 1607-1910*, New York: Scribner's and Sons, 1980.